An insider's guide . . .

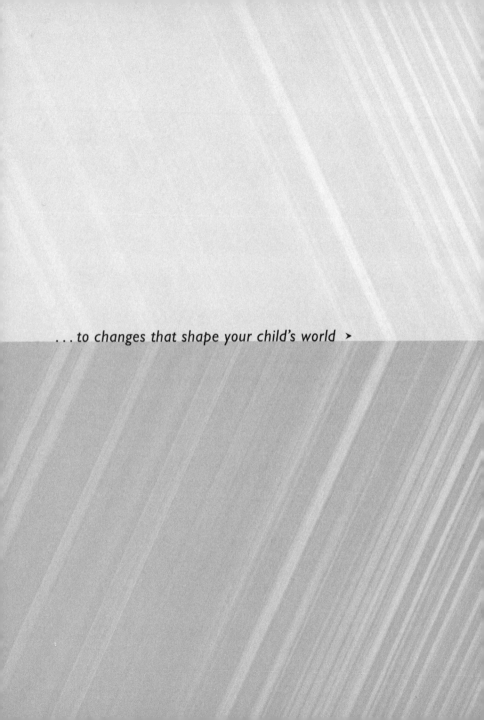

. . . to changes that shape your child's world ➤

FOCUS ON THE FAMILY®
R E S O U R C E S

TREND-SAVVY PARENTING

DR. MARY MANZ SIMON

Tyndale House Publishers
CAROL STREAM, ILLINOIS

Trend-Savvy Parenting
Copyright © 2006 by Dr. Mary Manz Simon
All rights reserved. International copyright secured.

A Focus on the Family book published by
Tyndale House Publishers, Carol Stream, Illinois 60188

TYNDALE is a registered trademark of Tyndale House Publishers, Inc. Tyndale's quill logo
is a trademark of Tyndale House Publishers, Inc.

Editors: Larry Weeden, Brandy Bruce
Cover design: Ron Kaufmann

Library of Congress Cataloging-in-Publication Data
Simon, Mary Manz, 1948-
    Trend-savvy parenting : an insider's guide to changes that shape your child's world / by
Dr. Mary Manz Simon.
        p. cm.
    "A Focus on the Family book."
    Includes bibliographical references.
    ISBN 10: 1-58997-134-5
    ISBN 13: 978-1-58997-134-9
    1. Christianity and culture. 2. Child rearing. 3. Parenting. I. Title.
    BR115.C8S565 2006
    248.8'45—dc22
                                                    2005026201

Printed in the United States of America
1 2 3 4 5 6 7 8 9 /11 10 09 08 07 06

for Hank

〉〉〉

My journey to becoming a trend tracker didn't begin at a marketing conference or in a publisher's boardroom. It began in a hospital, where I delivered three children in three and a half years.

All too soon, I realized my children were growing up in a whole new world. If I was going to walk alongside them, I needed to keep current with the culture. I talked with other parents, and I realized they, too, were hungry to know what was happening and how they could raise their children against the background of societal trends.

I am convinced that if we define the trends and talk about the implications and applications, parents will be helped in rearing a generation of happy, loving kids who will make this world a better place.

Mary Manz Simon

For more information about the author,
visit www.marymanzsimon.com.

〉〉〉

FREE Discussion Guide!
A discussion guide for Trend-Savvy Parenting is available at

ChristianBookGuides.com

Contents

Introduction

This book gave my computer a headache.

Spell-check never accepted Mousers and Rewinders as actual words. Of course, they are more than just words. They reflect major societal trends that are having an influence on the family.

Every generation has a generation gap. However, because of the accelerating pace of change, it's possible that more than a mere gap will emerge between parents and children. We are poised on the edge of a societal rift.

Some shifts are obvious: Any parent or child who shops for breakfast cereal observes that we live in a choice-mentality society. An onlooker on the sidelines of a select soccer game learns about competitive parenting. Other societal changes, which lurk beneath the lifestyle surface, are identified only by social historians. For example, a grandma who orders a doll that "looks just like my granddaughter" reflects a level of technology that permits incredible personalization and customization.

But it's not just the landscape that is changing at hyper speed: The mindscape is also changing. Parents are hit especially hard by these seismic shifts. Time starved and overwhelmed, parents struggle to simultaneously juggle the daily schedule, find a healthy balance, and raise happy, loving kids.

As we attempt to catch up with society, our self-esteem suffers.

Effectiveness decreases. A sense of defeat replaces the joy that can accompany the thrill, challenge, and privilege of raising the next generation.

However, understanding these concepts provides the framework to manage the outside influences that are shaping not just our children but an entire generation of families. That's why you now hold *Trend-Savvy Parenting*. This book will define the terms, identify why they matter, and provide practical applications for parenting on the frontlines. In addition, you'll hear from your peers as they face the same issues.

As a mother of three, I've lived in the parenting trenches. I know that moms and dads need easy access to practical advice. My personal experience, coupled with continual analysis of societal trends, has prompted me to share this information with other parents through speaking engagements, books and articles, and broadcast media.

The terms in this book reflect the fact that we are raising a brand-aware, media-savvy generation of multitaskers. But regardless of the challenges, we can be encouraged, equipped, and empowered.

Remember that we aren't alone in this journey. You are here for a purpose. You are here to parent in this twenty-first century. The God who made both you and your child wants to help you succeed.

So walk with me, as side by side we seek to understand what it means to parent in the shadow of ratings creep, cope with luxe kids, and find our way through Falloween.

 |

Age of Entitlement

> *What is it?*

The era in which our children are growing up.

> *Why should I care?*

Three elements morph together here: The first relates to development, the second to growing up in a high-tech world, and the third to our sinful human nature.

A baby thinks the world revolves around him. Or, you can say a baby is egocentric. That's often reflected in the emerging language of a toddler who says "I do it" or "Mine." A young child believes everyone and everything revolves around him. Gradually a child de-centers. The self-centeredness decreases as he begins to respect others and develop more adult-type logic, which allows him to mentally view the world from other perspectives. However, this natural de-centering process is being artificially delayed for children growing up in the current Age of Entitlement.

In previous generations, an "attitude" emerged when a 16 year old slid behind the wheel of a car. Today, an eight year old who fixes a glitch in the home entertainment system exudes a similar "attitude." Children live in a digital world, so going online is as natural as going outside to play. Helping Mom program the microwave is no big deal. Reprogramming the digital clock may challenge Grandpa, but it's easy for a nine year old. This high comfort level with technology fuels the notion of entitlement. Follow the logic: "Because I am a cool tech kid, I am entitled to . . ."

wear a trendy shirt.

stay up later.

door-to-door service to all my activities.

You might not fall for it, but even a young child may communicate, "You owe me." After all, this is the dawn of the Age of Entitlement. Generations of parents have taught both humility and compassion, but today, those efforts must be more intentional. This begins with helping a child identify and understand her own feelings. Once she can articulate how she feels, then she can express concern for others.

❭ What can I do?

1. Be the boundary-setter for your child. Even though an eight year old may be a tech wizard, he doesn't know how to set an appropriate bedtime or live within a budget. Your focus is to provide a healthy, nurtur-

ing, safe environment. Because you are the expert—not your child—don't hesitate to set and enforce appropriate boundaries.

2. Expect polite behavior every day. This means you teach common courtesy. Social graces have fallen through the cracks of our hyper-speed world. Take every opportunity to model caring behavior: open a door for someone, carry a load of groceries, say "please" and "thank you."

3. Integrate empathy into daily life. Empathy—understanding situations from another point of view—can reduce self-centeredness. Even the simple question, "How do you think your friend will feel if he's not invited?" encourages a child to look beyond himself.

4. Help a child develop compassion. We're surrounded by opportunities to show care for someone who is in trouble or who made a mistake. If you discuss playground-bullying issues, talk about how words and actions can hurt someone. Volunteer as a family to deliver food to a local shelter. Selective exposure to people in need and alertness to the less fortunate can help a child de-center.

Some children are naturally more self-centered than others. These children may get easily frustrated when they do something wrong. Some

〉〉〉

Raising a child in today's affluent middle class is a definite challenge. When our son saw a friend with the newest hot toy or video game, he let us know that he should have one as well. He wasn't obnoxious about it, but the expectation was clear.

—Larry, father of one

children resist or refuse to learn from a mistake. Especially for these children, link words with caring behaviors. For example, compliment a child who lets his friend choose a cookie first. Thank a child for holding the umbrella above the baby's stroller. Your verbal acknowledgment affirms a child for his concern and validates his action.

However, avoid giving a child additional rewards for donating time at the animal shelter or serving as a church nursery aide. A child needs to become sensitive to how he feels—inside—when he's helpful. Over time, and with repeated experiences, a child will begin to identify the intangible rewards that are built into caring behaviors. When this happens, the influence of growing up in the Age of Entitlement will start to fade and be replaced by genuine empathy, humility, and compassion.

2

Brawlgames

> ## What is it?

Children's sport competitions at which parents display inappropriate behavior.

> ## Why should I care?

When parents carry a lawn chair plus an overdose of emotional intensity onto the sidelines of a child's activity, the game can disintegrate into a brawlgame. Sometimes parents heckle or taunt players, coaches, or officials. Other parents grumble about players or bad-mouth referees after questionable calls. Occasionally, physical violence explodes. Parents who show unsportsmanlike conduct may be ejected, or their child's team may forfeit the game. But in every instance, children have been exposed to inappropriate adult behavior.

As a result of high-profile brawlgames, some leagues now hold mandatory parent-sensitivity sessions before a season begins. Other sport groups develop and then strictly enforce rules contained in a sport parent code of ethics or handbook. Some leagues distribute a parent handbook with specific rules of conduct. Such efforts frequently pay off in more appropriate parent behavior.

〉 What can I do?

Focus on fun, not winning. This is a challenge for parents, especially dads, who typically have a dramatically different perspective on the purpose of sports than their children. When asked, "Why do you want to play?" young children typically answer, "I want to wear the uniform." Older kids often join a team because their friends play. An older, highly gifted athlete might play to improve skills, build a resume, or because he likes the sport and loves to play. When parents, especially dads, are asked, "Why do you want your child to play?" the honest answer is straightforward: to win. A brawlgame typically erupts when parents on the sidelines believe children should win at all costs.

Regardless of the actual reason a child joins a team, having fun and winning are both more likely when a child has the fundamental skills for the game. Too often, a child is dropped into a game situation, complete with uniforms, cheerleaders, and rules, but lacks the ability to bounce, kick, or catch a ball. Because some children enter organized sports at such an early age, they aren't even sure what to do with a ball if they see one. A focus on skill development, especially during the early years, reduces frustration for the player and the potential of a brawlgame.

Parents can informally teach a variety of skills without the stress of an organized game. For example, toddlers and parents can toss or roll a big inflatable ball, indoors or out, as a first step to baseball. Preschoolers move up to using a broad plastic or sponge bat and ball. Five year olds like to run, so they can chase around makeshift bases made of masking tape. Because children at this age focus on the physical act of running without tripping, it's difficult for them to comprehend rules, too. So instead of labeling the bases, try running with your child so he naturally learns to go around a diamond in the proper direction.

Beginning at age six or seven, children are ready to hit a ball off a tee. Continue to play catch and scoop up grounders, remembering that the purpose is to have fun. Even if your child never wears a baseball uniform, he's learned fundamental skills that can be applied to many physical activities.

A parent who teaches a child basic motor skills may also reduce the potential of losing his own temper. This parent has followed his child from the very first ball toss. He knows how hard his child worked to

〉〉〉

"Brawlgames," plain and simple, are the reason I'm not coaching soccer anymore. Basically, you've got some parents looking at six and seven year olds as if they were high schoolers, even going so far as considering hiring coaches to develop skilled players. I'm still coaching softball, but it's truly because of the supportive group of parents I am working with.

—Christopher, father of three

learn how to kick a soccer ball without falling down. This coaching parent should have a healthy focus on the child, not the score of the game.

However, if you would benefit from learning about conflict resolution or would like help in anger management before attending your child's games, locate local clinics. These are commonly held for referees, coaches, and umpires, but are now often open to parents as well. Training focuses on defusing potential brawlgames and building skills related to positive coaching. Many of the principles are applicable to parent-child situations beyond the sports arena.

Brawlgames are preventable. There is no place for unsportsmanlike conduct at any children's event. If hostility or violence simmers, parents should remove themselves from the scene, cool down, and return later to support their child, his team, and his coach.

3

Cause Marketing

› What is it?

The process of informing customers that corporate donations are being given from profits.

› Why should I care?

Cause marketing was awakened on September 11, 2001. To support people affected by the tragedy and bolster relief efforts, corporations donated huge amounts of money, product, and employee time. During the post-9/11 era, companies learned that both children and adults liked to help others through their purchases. Today, cause marketing has been embraced as an *almost* painless way to contribute to the common good.

Because children are immediately linked to world events through the Internet, they are increasingly aware of issues and causes. Research shows that teens know that even distant events may affect everyday life.[1] This is good, because today's children are optimistic. Marketing experts know this, and that's why cause marketing is sometimes targeted directly to children, who are purely motivated to help others. However, children do not always make wise choices regarding cause marketing simply due to their inexperience and lack of maturity. For example, a child might spend allowance money on a toy at a specific store, because billboards show the store "gives back" to the community. A five year old cannot see through the corporate greed that may determine a mere one-half of 1 percent of profits is donated to a worthy agency. By the time kids reach their teens, they should be able to differentiate between legitimate cause marketing and suggestive selling, which is when the product cost is hiked to camouflage the corporate donation.

⟩ What should I do?

Model a balanced approach to cause marketing. Too often, a child may convince a parent to purchase a specific cereal because the box highlights

---

⟩ ⟩ ⟩

The credit union that issues our primary credit card gives a part of its profits to charity, a fact that's advertised on the front of the card. My younger son noticed the wording and asked about it. I explained that this was one reason we used that card. He thought that was "cool!"

Howard, father of three

a social agency partner. This is an ideal time to explain that you can't contribute to every worthy cause. Also, discuss the various techniques you apply to disciplined shopping. For example, if you have a $15 budget for a birthday gift, ask your child to find a gift, card, and wrapping paper within that limit. When shopping, ask your child to read the grocery list as you walk through the store. Some parents add a line for discretionary purchases or donations.

Look for cause marketing campaigns that involve a gift of time or effort. For example, a fast-food outlet may sponsor an art contest where the winning child's drawing will result in a donation to the student's school. This type of participation demonstrates that a child's time, talents, and abilities can also help others.

〉〉〉

My 12-year-old daughter noticed that the pharmacy we use was supporting hurricane victims. For every paper stocking we bought, a dollar went to a relief organization. She pulled out a dollar and wrote her name on a stocking. Kids are learning early that they can get involved, too!

Jill, mother of three

〉〉〉 4

Competitive Parent

〉 *What does it mean?*

A person who is driven to stay "ahead of the curve."

〉 *Why should I care?*

Early in the twenty-first century, the "get-ahead–stay-ahead" corporate strategy spilled over into family life. This competitive streak among parents is triggered by an underlying need for affirmation. Parents have always craved affirmation because we live with delayed gratification. We spend years wondering if cheering on the sidelines of muddy fields and attending parent-teacher conferences will result in a child who "turns out." In the past, a closely knit, multi-generational family structure gave encouragement, nurture, and support. That direct support structure has evaporated.

As a result, the competitive parent has emerged. Boasting about a child's accomplishments or urging performance beyond what's healthy gives a resounding "yes" to the recurring, yet unspoken question, "Am I a good parent?"

Competition among parents often simmers beneath the surface of polite conversation. Competition first emerges even before the birth of a child when casual conversation turns to topics which have the potential to separate parents by their choices. Common early-stage topics focus on two issues: food delivery and parenting style (breast-feeding vs. bottle-feeding and stay-at-home mom vs. employed mom). The unannounced "winner" varies with the specific social circle or situation. For example, in the waiting room of a pediatrician who encourages breast-feeding, a mom who nurses her 18-month-old daughter may be the unofficial victor. The competitive parent may whisper to herself, "I'm going to nurse even *longer*."

Later, the focus shifts to the child. At developmental landmarks or skill markers, a competitive parent builds himself up by tearing others down. For example, a mom might say to another preschool parent, "My son started reading a year ago. Is *your* daughter reading yet?"

❭ What can I do?

Prideful behavior lurks around the edges of a child's achievements, but we can take two child-focused actions to avoid becoming a competitive parent:

1. Applaud a child's attempts, not just successes. Genuine praise is honest and appropriate.

2. Joyfully celebrate a child's milestones as blessings.

We can also reduce the need for affirmation via our child's accomplishments by building a meaningful support system. Intentionally connect with these three types of people:

A parent with a child older than yours. Catch a glimpse of the future from this person. Learn about issues this parent faces. Ask how she solves her problems. Then think ahead and ask yourself, "How will I handle this situation when my child is this age?" This proactive approach builds confidence in the ability to parent effectively.

A peer parent. Affirmation comes from this parent by merely seeing that others deal with similar issues. A peer parent helps put everyday issues into a big picture, and you will walk away with a broader view of situations. As a result, you realize, "I'm not the only one dealing with a 10 year old who wants to dress like a teenager."

A parent with a younger child. Every parent should teach other parents. There's a new generation of parents following right behind you. It's your turn to teach. You are affirmed when you share helpful advice and ideas that work—not from a position of perfection, but with an empathetic heart and listening ear.

〉〉〉

The competitive edge in parents can almost take on a prideful nature. It's not just being proud of our children, but it reaches the point of "My child is better than yours and I'm going to prove it!"

Paula, mother of two

Using a support system reminds us that most parents are trying to meet the same goal: to raise happy, loving children who will be contributing members of society. A support system emphasizes the similarities, not differences, among parents. Helping others—and accepting help ourselves—diffuses the competitive spirit.

Crib Scholar

› What is it?

An infant or toddler who is subjected to multiple stimuli, whether or not developmentally appropriate, with the intent to grow the baby's brain.

› Why should I care?

Recent advancements in technology have allowed scientists to study brain development with noninvasive techniques. Studies have validated what earlier research indicated: Brain development in the early years lays the foundation for lifelong growth.

We know that babies are born with billions of brain cells. However, the connections (synapses) between these cells are incomplete at birth. The synapses grow when stimulated. This growth is fast and intense during the first three years of life.

Parents who hear about the importance of early childhood stimulation tend to apply two twenty-first century notions:

1. Fast is good, but faster is better.

2. More is good, but even more is better.

However, neither assumption takes a comprehensive approach to child development. Yet even in this book, we see instances where this is happening. Have you seen a computer mouse in the shape of a baby animal, ergonomically designed to fit the hand of a toddler? Has your two year old used lapware? Today, video games present very early learning skills so toddlers feel like they're playing just like an older sibling.

As you help your child grow, stay alert to problems with the underlying "drop down" concept of crib scholars. Children's books are a common example: A popular picture book suddenly appears in board book format. Why? The assumption is that what's good literature for a six year old is even better for a baby. The underlying idea is to "drop down"

> > >

When our five year old was a baby, he would sit with me while I was at the keyboard. Drew learned to type his whole name, his phone number, and his address before he could write any of it. Now that Drew is at preschool, the computer is his favorite activity center. It kind of scares me that he knows so much about it. But when he's a little older, maybe I won't have to call the computer tech who charges $75 an hour. I'll just ask my son for help.

Rhonda, mother of one

concepts for older children so that babies can learn faster. But think carefully before you embrace the "downward creep" of playpen sports or apply the "Mozart effect" to stimulate brain development.

Instead, refocus on what babies actually need. Infants need a safe, loving environment to build initial trust relationships. They need attention to their physical needs. They need consistent, caring adults to hold, cuddle, and talk to them. For example, a baby uses his eyes to learn about the world. In the early weeks, he notices movement and strong contrast between light and dark. This is the reason some toys sold for newborns are black and white shapes that move. However, when Mom comes into the room, she also moves. And because newborns prefer their mother's voice, baby turns to listen. Mom picks up baby. A newborn's sensitivity to touch is well developed, so baby feels Mom's soothing stroke.

In that single motion of Mom walking toward the crib, baby watches with his eyes, hears with his ears, and feels a soothing touch. That's multisensory stimulation. That's what grows the synapses in a baby's brain.

〉 What can I do?

Every parent wants his or her baby to get a head start, but use these guidelines to give your child a *smart* start:

1. Your child's timeline may differ from that of other babies. If your baby is within range of developmental landmarks but walks three months after your neighbor's toddler, that's all right. Your baby is not in a race to the finish line. If you have a question or concern, don't lie awake worrying; talk with your pediatrician.

2. Let your baby celebrate his age. A one year old does not need to dress like a two year old or sleep in a nursery with alphabet posters. All too soon, you will tell your teen to "act your age" and "dress your age." Those are helpful reminders for you at this stage of a child's development.

3. Your baby may look like she's developing really fast, then suddenly slow down. That's normal, because different parts of the brain grow at different rates. For example, a three month old may be fascinated by a mobile turning above the crib. During this time, a baby may seem to make little progress toward sitting up. That's because he's working hard on sensory integration, which means he's combining the image of that mobile with the music he hears when the mobile turns.

4. Your baby needs an interesting environment. Playing with her is good. Tickle her toes; sing rhymes and lullabies. However, stay alert to signs that she's tired. If your baby starts to fuss, cry, or look away, she is tired of playing crib scholar and needs recess. Finding a healthy balance should begin in infancy.

5. Don't be fooled by sophisticated ads and marketing hooks. Be open to learning about child development, but most of all, relax and enjoy your baby.

>>> 6

Customization

> *What is it?*

A public expression of "Who I am."

> *Why should I care?*

Customization has been called the "ultimate" self-expression. We "say it my way" in the latte we drink, the hood ornament that decorates our car, and in the ring tones we program into our cell phones. Customization follows a generic developmental timeline. This begins to escalate when the "it's mine" of the early childhood years shifts to "I'm me" for tweens. In their search for independence, 8 to 12 year olds have always looked for ways to distinguish being a "big kid" from being a "mere child." Today, that characteristic is emerging in customization. There's a simple reason: Technology has made personalization quick and affordable.

Today, an 11 year old may get brackets for his braces that match the color of his baseball team, or a 12 year old may design a notebook cover that "sings" with a sound chip. These are common ways to customize. But those trendy looks come with a bonus: They communicate a "grown-up" image to others. Older tweens and teens bask in the peer attention that comes with customization because they like to be noticed. Children have typically showcased their personalities through small accessories like jewelry and backpack chains. Today's extreme tweens and teens have taken that a step further to include tattoos and body piercing.

As a child customizes everything from braces to bikes, he begins to define who he is. Because tech-based personalization is often inexpensive, a child can also try out a variety of messages about who he thinks he's becoming, who he'd like to be, or what fits his personal style at the moment. That's why a child might have five totally different styles of music in her iPod.

〉〉〉

My daughter, Brianna, is 17, and the huge thing for her and her friends is customization through the Web. These teens use Web sites and Internet blogs to post pictures and links to their favorite Web sites, keep online journals, and get feedback from their friends. These Web sites and blogs can be quite personal; parents need to closely monitor their kids' online activity to make sure their children aren't giving away too much information.

Bruce, father of two

Children who embrace customization have launched a product category called "roomwares." Even preschoolers can choose paint hues that are child-friendly. Home improvement stores host do-it-yourself seminars that attract older kids and their parents. As a result, every inch of a child's room can reflect his individuality. Décor, though, is merely one reflection of customization.

❯ What can I do?

The kid-culture definition of "cool" changes by the minute. Younger children, who are strongly influenced by trends in pop culture, may want an entire room to reflect the newest Hollywood release. If you choose to integrate pop culture elements into décor, choose inexpensive elements like throw pillows, or let your child get creative with easy-to-remove appliqués or peel-off stickers.

Tweens and teens often avoid ready-made furnishings. To these kids, personalizing implies creating a look that's unique. Unfortunately, this is achieved only by shopping at numerous stores. Begin by setting a spending limit. Visit bargain outlets or resale stores. Off-mall shopping fits a lower budget and matches these older kids who want to customize. The buying process may be tedious to you but important to your child.

Steer your child toward safe personalization. You might need to be protective as your child seeks to be expressive. Avoid products like backpacks and umbrellas that publicize your child's name. Hang the customized license plate on the bedroom ceiling instead.

Children place a high value on customizing their room. Although parents want children to be comfortable, clearly communicate to what degree personal space can be customized. Some parents only invite a child to make decisions about design elements that are reversible. Some children share the cost. Customizing space or personalizing clothing may be acceptable ways for children to define themselves, but parents may still need to set limits.

7

Cyber Bullying

〉 What is it?

High-tech harassment, often anonymous.

〉 Why should I care?

Technology has made it possible for bullies to penetrate even the safest places for children. When a hateful comment appears on an Internet chat room screen, a child may face lies about him that floated through cyberspace. Rumors can be spread through text messages sent to screens of friends, neighbors, and classmates. A cell phone with a digital camera allows bullies to take and transmit potentially embarrassing photos. This can escalate into cyberstalking when photos are posted on Web sites. And all of these dirty tricks can be done anonymously. The implication is obvious: A "friend" might be the cyber bully.

High-tech harassment is not new, but the impact is growing. The number of entry points for bullies has increased as the number of portals has expanded. One ironic twist to security issues is that parents who purchase a cell phone for their child's safety also open another channel for bullying.

Technologically advanced cyber bullying presents a difficult dilemma for parents. For example, a cell phone is tough to monitor. Tweens view phones as a symbol of independence. Teens resent parental interference (see "Tech Tether"). So in spite of their vulnerability via the cell, tweens and teens vigorously defend their phones. As a result, few moms and dads unplug a child or use highly sensitive digital surveillance systems.

⟩ ⟩ ⟩

When our 15-year-old babysitter, Jennifer, broke up with her boyfriend, she thought that the relationship was over. Far from it. In the months that followed, the ex-boyfriend sent Jennifer threatening and vulgar e-mails. Jennifer changed her log-in names, but usually within days he would find her new addresses. When she tried to prove that this young man was cyber-stalking using the school computers, the high-school officials found the evidence inconclusive. Jennifer got the most help from a software package that screened her incoming e-mails.

Margaret, mother of three

Some parents may never even know about high-tech harassment. There's an emerging twenty-first century version of a code of silence: What's online stays online. Parents who wonder why their child is out of sorts might not even suspect cyber bullying.

Although victims may never see or identify the cyber bully, this form of harassment can be as harmful as other forms of schoolyard taunts. Yet some school officials are hesitant to become involved. One stated reason: concern about the line between First Amendment rights for a cyber bully and the protection of a victim. Another reason is the difficulty in proving that cyber bullying happens during school hours, on school grounds, using school equipment. Other school administrators have a completely different perspective. They want to know about anything that affects students. More uniform policies will eventually emerge with increasing awareness of the problem.

〉 What can I do?

Because cyber bullies are so hard to track and the harassment can be so devastating, prevention is the best solution. This is the reason children should limit online contacts to a small circle of friends. This is a special challenge in schools and geographic regions where an extensive address book is a social status symbol. This happens most commonly among teens. Your child should personally know every individual in his online address book. A parent who regularly reviews an address book with a child has an opportunity to learn about the child's friends and delete names when appropriate. Children should also guard their cell phone number and any other personal door that opens on the high-tech high-way. Parents must teach children to draw a line between public and private information.

Children should not respond to negative or hurtful messages. Some counselors advise that on the playground and online, children should walk away from a bully. Most educators recommend blocking messages from the sender after copies of e-mails or chat room conversations are printed for documentation. When inappropriate messages are forwarded to a Web service provider or phone company, the company may suggest contacting local law enforcement agencies. Information about new harassment procedures is sometimes included on billing statements, the company Web site, or the phone book. However, guidelines and recommendations are still evolving. Procedures for handling inappropriate messages and recommendations for victims are continually being updated.

Children should be encouraged to develop real-time relationships. This happens naturally when daily screen time is limited. Also, parents who volunteer to chauffeur children and host events for their friends demonstrate support of face-to-face socialization. Building personal relationships that are caring, forgiving, and loving provides a direct contrast to flat-screen acquaintances.

Be aware of signs that indicate your child may have a problem with a cyber bully. Children who are targeted by a cyber bully may hesitate to answer their cell phone. Victims might avoid going online or check e-mail only when no one is watching. They may prefer solitary activities because they are afraid to trust even close friends. Victims may also have typical stress-related symptoms including sleep problems, irritability, and stomachaches.

Being mean has become easier as technology has advanced. Underground harassment will continue until victims, parents, educators, law enforcement, and members of the judicial system work together to solve the problem.

8

Edutainment

〉 What is it?

Media with the potential to teach and entertain.

〉 Why should I care?

Education has combined with entertainment to become "edutainment." Other terms, including *entertainment education* (E-E), *infotainment,* and *technotainment* have slightly different shades of meaning, but are sometimes used interchangeably. *Educon* refers specifically to education on TV.

In edutainment, the lure of pure entertainment has merged with the promise of learning. We see this in word games on cereal boxes, quizzes on theme park maps, and a record number of families participating at interactive exhibits in science centers, museums, and zoos. Malls even advertise "edutainment centers." The potential for learning is often integrated into children's leisure environments and activities.

Why is this happening? Because our world changes so fast, learning is the only way to keep up.

To emphasize the importance of lifelong learning, educators selectively use edutainment to "hook" students to discover the joy of learning. In schools, edutainment usually comes packaged as computer software. These teaching tools are especially helpful as students reinforce skills, expand learning, and grow the higher-level critical thinking skills of analysis, synthesis, and evaluation. Teachers have always incorporated these goals into learning objectives, but today, sophisticated software can accelerate, extend, and enrich the process.

With the shrinking of school budgets, software can even substitute for programs that have been cut. For example, children can create artwork on a computer screen instead of using charcoal, tempera, and watercolors. The hands-on and virtual experiences are different, but students are still being exposed to artistic expression.

> > >

When I watch my two year old singing a song on TV that is teaching her letter sounds, it sometimes gives me goose bumps. I see that she is being educated on how to speak and later how to read. These educational tools are a major plus to my wife and me.

David, father of one

However, critics caution that edutainment is creating a new problem: electronic illiteracy, or "e-literacy." Children might "tune out" unless sophisticated multi-sensory fun is integrated into lessons. Some teachers feel that they have to entertain to teach effectively. Others are concerned that the point and click approach to learning is more appealing than hands-on instruction which includes verbal expression and interaction with classmates. Some educators complain that students who spend long periods of time in front of screens have shorter attention spans. Research indicates that rapidly changing images may trigger problems with focusing, but more study is needed.

Parents who place a high value on learning (see chapters on "Crib Scholar" and "Mousers") may appreciate edutainment as a babysitter with a plus: A child learns while he has fun. Edutainment may even be one of the criteria a parent uses when choosing television programs, software, and DVDs.

However, researchers are still studying how the "stealth learning" or "embedded learning" of edutainment affects children's mental processing, content retention, and patterns of communication. For example,

> ⟩ ⟩ ⟩
>
> *Edutainment didn't come along soon enough for me. None of my children were the sit-still-and-listen-to-a-lecture type of learners. Video games and computer software have been very helpful, especially with my third child.*
>
> Deb, mother of three

what is the optimal length of educon for children at various ages? At what stage of the instructional process does edutainment have the strongest impact: Introduction of new material? Instruction in new skills? Practice of skills that requires repetition? Until we have more answers, moderation should guide purchase.

⟩ What can I do?

Edutainment is available in many formats, but computer software is the most common form used at home and at school. Packaging and advertising material often highlight three important elements:

1. Interactivity. Children learn by being mentally and physically active. Look for opportunities for your child to respond with more than a click. Key word: action.

2. Content. Look for subject areas that interest your child or skills he needs to practice. Key words: age appropriate.

3. Long-term use. To avoid the isolation that results from computer use, look for tech toys that can be used by you *and* your child. Also look for software that will grow up with your child. Key word: levels.

These three characteristics of edutainment software have high appeal to parents and children. The potential of raising a bright child appeals to parents, and cutting-edge fun attracts kids. But parents must continually balance the use of tech toys with hands-on learning and fun.

9

Falloween

> ## 》 What is it?

The non-stop commercial season that links back-to-school (BTS), Halloween, Thanksgiving, and Christmas.

> ## 》 Why should I care?

We only need to enter a store in autumn to see how this new season morphs together previously freestanding holidays: plaid, pumpkins, Pilgrims, and Christmas trees are displayed in adjacent areas. But the impact of the obvious holiday blur is not limited to the cash register.

In the past, we emotionally progressed, step by step, through autumn to early winter. We marked the changing of the seasons with distinct rituals. We celebrated traditions for each holiday.

We shopped for notebooks and pencils, toasted marshmallows over a bonfire, rode a hay wagon out to a pumpkin field, smelled the turkey baking, and finally began our march to the manger. We paused at each point. Memories connected the past and the present. Instead of rushing at hyper speed, as we now do on a daily basis, we stopped and focused on the meaning and message of each holiday. Merely thinking about those holidays generates a feeling of nostalgia for the "good old days."

That's because we've lost them.

Now that these dates have merged together in one massive Christmas prequel, we've lost the psychological anchoring of the individual dates. In the past, holidays offered the opportunity to step back from daily activities. Today, there's an undercurrent of "rushing the season," although we're uncertain of exactly what season we are celebrating.

We're also in danger of losing the most important holiday of the season: Christmas. A drive toward inclusivity means that some schools now offer winter break at the end of December instead of Christmas vacation. School programs feature reindeer instead of anything or anyone connected with the manger. Even the traditional greeting, "Merry Christmas," has been replaced by the politically correct, "Seasons Greet-

> > >

Thanksgiving has such a rich history, but it's being overlooked. I want my daughter to be grateful for the new life she has in America, while being mindful of her Chinese heritage and thankful for the life her biological mother gave her.

Carol, mother of one

ings" or "Happy Holidays." A cynic looking at the Falloween scene might comment, "We rush through autumn only to end with an empty Christmas."

〉 What can I do?

Throughout Falloween, look for opportunities to celebrate the distinctiveness of each holiday. If traditions truly are the glue that hold families together across time and space, claim certain annual rituals to anchor your family.

For example, you might want to consider:

BTS: Launch the new school year with a formal dinner sometime during the week before school starts. Use a tablecloth and napkin rings. Arrange flowers for a centerpiece. Eat in the dining room. Focus on hopes and dreams for the coming months.

Autumn: Celebrate the uniqueness of fall in your area. Help children design a leaf house on the front lawn. Visit a farm that offers hay

---

〉〉〉

Why would I want to rush through fall and the beauty of that season? Why would I want to pass up all the opportunities to teach God's love at Thanksgiving? As my own personal statement, I have tried to avoid making Christmas purchases before Thanksgiving. Yet sometimes I feel that I'm doing the rushing, too.

Janis, mother of one

rides. Walk through a forest preserve to see how animals prepare for winter.

Halloween: Participate in a fall festival at your church, park, or community center. Visit a pumpkin patch and then have fun carving a pumpkin together.

Thanksgiving: Put five kernels of corn into muffin cups at each place on the holiday table, symbolic of the hard winter faced by the Pilgrims. Go around the table five times, asking each person to share a blessing for which he or she is thankful.

Christmas: Before children open the daily window on Advent calendars, light the appropriate candles on the Advent wreath. Ask a family member to choose a favorite carol or seasonal hymn that you can sing together; take turns from day to day. On Christmas Eve, have the oldest person present read the story of Luke 2 from the Bible.

Continue to look for traditions that can grow up with your children. For example, young children can sprinkle colorful decorations on holiday cookies; older children can mix the batter; teens can take charge of holiday baking. These activities, and your existing rituals, will help your family-focused celebrations emerge as anchors when the pace accelerates near the end of each year.

 10

Gamepad Dads

› What is it?

Fathers who play video games with their children.

› Why should I care?

Dads are meeting their children at video game screens. In the entertainment software industry, these men are identified as gamepad dads. Social history analysts expected this new demographic would emerge. After all, today's fathers played video games when they were boys, so they view gaming as part of family entertainment.

Gamepad dads represent a uniquely twenty-first century parent-child bonding opportunity. The screen is a neutral and compelling meeting ground for fathers and their children. This is true whether or not they have a strong emotional connection.

Video games have a high coolness factor, something that appeals to both dads and kids. The dazzling, complex, hyper-speed, three-dimensional graphics with sophisticated sound effects rival anything seen on the big screen. The physical closeness to a video screen pulls players into exciting environments and challenging situations. Video games are an easy way for dads and their children to have fun together. "Gray gamers," or grandfathers, offer cross-generational play options.

Dads who grew up with video games know that relationships can be built at screens. Gaming with Dad is a wonderful opportunity for socialization, especially for younger children, who spend significant amounts of time playing video games alone. Gaming with Dad can also be important during preadolescence, when some tweens become secretive. Children who were open communicators at age eight may close up at age 12. Playing in cyberspace offers the opportunity to reconnect in real time.

Researchers are only beginning to study issues relevant to the video game arena. Gamepad dads need to stay alert to ongoing studies about the addictive nature of game playing, the link to childhood obesity, and the behavioral impact of playing games with violent and aggressive plots.

But are there gamepad moms? Not yet, but that might be changing.

The majority of video game players are men. Current first generation games have been action oriented with predominantly male leading characters. Moms have traditionally preferred games with a storyline and some strong female characters. As the video game market matures, developers may capitalize on these preferences, simply to grow the market. If that happens, gamepad moms might be the next major demographic to emerge.

Of course, not every father is a gamepad dad. Playing video games should never substitute for teaching children how to bait a hook or locate Orion in the night sky. Being a gamepad dad is only one potential element of twenty-first century fathering.

〉 What can I do?

Gamepad dads must help children maintain a healthy balance between the screen and other activities. For example, a dad who promises to meet his son "at the screen" should also set aside time to shoot hoops and visit the library. An appropriate screen limit should be set and enforced as soon as a child begins gaming, because habits become more difficult to change as children grow up.

Fathers who sit next to their children are perfectly situated to watch a child's reaction to a game and response to virtual situations. Whenever possible, gamepad dads should transfer screen learning to real life. For example, if a virtual wagon train family faces a food shortage, Dad can

〉〉〉

Playing at the computer has always been a daddy thing in our house. I remember being in the kitchen while my husband was trying to teach Joshua a new game. About every eight seconds, you could hear Joshua ask, "Can I try that, Daddy?" or "Can I do that?" I finally peeked my head around the corner and asked with a smile, "Whose game is that, anyway?"

Janis, mother of one

highlight ways the characters were resourceful in finding food. Or Dad might note how different characters approached the problem, adding, "I did something similar when . . ."

Gamepad dads and their children can also look together for games they'd like to play. Most libraries have extensive video game collections. Sampling games before buying them offers an excellent model of fiscal responsibility. When shopping, gamepad dads can talk about judging appropriateness by using both the printed rating system and a personal value system. This is especially important during the tween years. Research shows that 8 to 12 year olds want to know what parents think. Selecting a new game is an ideal time to talk about boundaries, priorities, and making choices.

Dads might notice that their preadolescent sons, especially, crave activities that give them a rush of power. These guys often get emotionally involved in screentime. They get a tremendous thrill by controlling figures on a screen. Dads can use these virtual reality situations to discuss power, control, competition, and intimidation. These themes become increasingly important as tweens move into the teen years. Defining the issues with initial discussions lays the foundation for future conversations.

 11

God Factor

⟩ What is it?

Heightened visibility of spirituality in society.

⟩ Why should I care?

Spirituality soared in the post-9/11 era. Public response to the best-selling *The Prayer of Jabez, The Purpose-Driven Life,* and the *Left Behind* series, along with the high-profile releases of *The Passion of the Christ* and *The Chronices of Narnia: The Lion, the Witch and the Wardrobe,* reflected an underlying search for meaning. Controversies raged over the faith of George W. Bush and his judicial appointees, the role of "values voters," the nature of Islam, and the public display of the Ten Commandments.

"God talk" even shows up in conversations on elementary school playgrounds. Questions about faith, death, and the afterlife regularly pop up among children in Internet chat rooms and bulletin boards.

When people talk about religious faith, it's good news if they're attracted to beliefs you agree with, or if it gives you an opportunity to discuss faith (which is sometimes hard to bring up) with your child. There's also a danger that your child might be attracted to beliefs you reject.

One way or the other, your child's own faith *is* being affected by all these discussions and controversies in the public arena.

⟩ What can I do?

As suggested above, you can use this trend as an opportunity to talk about faith and reinforce your values with your child. In my family's case, we're Christians. That means we're convinced (among other things) that in order to be in a right relationship with God, we have to believe that Jesus is His Son and that He died on the cross to pay the price for our sins, then was resurrected. Whether or not a person believes this determines his eternal destiny.

⟩ ⟩ ⟩

Whatever its other merits or drawbacks, TV does give parents plenty of opportunities to discuss spiritual matters with a child. After watching a show with my son, I would often ask him, "What did the character seem to believe about God?" or "How were people of faith portrayed in that program?"

Larry, father of one

So here's what I'd do if I still had a young child at home (mine are all grown) when, for example, a deadly natural disaster like Hurricane Katrina occurs. As we watched the news reports and appeals for aid together, I would talk about how this gave us a chance to help others in practical ways (money, food, etc.). But I would also discuss how uncertain life can be, as it proved to be for the Katrina victims, and how we need to be sure that we're ready spiritually for whatever life brings.

But does this trend also pose a threat to your child? Are you concerned, for instance, that you might need to shield your child from being preyed upon by celebrities and others promoting questionable beliefs? Suppose, for instance, that your child sees a famous entertainer promote unorthodox religious views on a TV program.

Here's how I would handle the situation, again from my perspective as a Christian: First, I'd emphasize to my child that he or she is always welcome to come to me with questions about anything heard at school, on TV, or on the Web. Second, I would do enough research (in books, the Web, by talking to my pastor) that I could explain to my child—in terms he or she could understand—how this other faith differs from our family's faith, and why those differences are important—why we're convinced that Christianity is the best understanding of God and how He wants us to relate to Him.

When questions about faith arise with a child, we need to answer them honestly and clearly, realizing that he or she is simply curious about spiritual matters, probably because of something heard that day at school or in the media.

Generally speaking, this trend is a great opportunity for people of faith. Examine your own beliefs and choose to reinforce in your child those that are most important. This can be an opportunity for both of you to grow spiritually.

>>> 12

Insulated Kids

> *What is it?*

Children who are protected from failure or problems through phony praise, rewards, or parental indulgence.

> *Why should I care?*

A positive self-image contributes to confidence. Children who feel good about themselves are more likely to accept challenges and avoid problem behaviors. Often, they are able to recover faster and more completely after facing tough situations. They are happier than children with a negative self-image.

Honest praise for a job well done contributes to a healthy view of self. For example, you boost self-esteem when you compliment a child who faithfully takes out the garbage without being asked. Letting children work through problems to find solutions also contributes to a positive self-image. But that's where some parents get snagged. Moms may find it less stressful to rescue a child than to see her struggle. Dads might want to "make life easier" for their children. Parents who have the time, opportunity, and money to smooth the road for their children ask the logical question, "Why not?"

The answer: insulated kids. Some children grow up without ever facing disappointment, doing household chores, or learning to organize their homework. They've been overprotected by well-intentioned parents who want to help. This isn't just happening at home. Some schools are discouraging competitive games that could result in hurt feelings. And some educators are even being advised to use alternatives to the red pen; red corrections might be inferred as demeaning.[1] But when adults help too much, children get hurt.

A common example is trophy overload. Shelves may sag under the weight of participation statues a girl "earned" on elementary school teams, but that same girl may have a rude awakening about her skill level when she does not qualify for the varsity team in high school. Or, a parent tells a teen, "You don't need to get a summer job. You've worked hard at school." Two years later, the now twenty-something scrambles to prepare for his first job interview. He's at a disadvantage because others competing for the same position are experienced in the work world.

Insulation from issues and the resulting lack of self-reliance contributes to a growing number of "boomerang kids," or those who return to live at home after college graduation. As a result, many young adults have a longer adolescence and postpone making difficult life decisions.

Insulation is not directly related to money. Overprotected kids are found in many homes of modest means, and conversely, children who live in the lap of luxury can do chores, contribute to the common good of the family, respect the work ethic, and have a healthy sense of self.

〉 What can I do?

1. Give honest praise. Even before children learn to read, they read emotions. This means a four year old can tell the difference between fake and honest comments. He will see through the lie, "That's the most beautiful painting you've ever made." Next time the preschooler is praised, he may wonder, *Is it really my best work?* Repeated empty praise can erode trust. In contrast, a four year old who hears, "Wow. You used a lot of peach. Did you know that's one of my favorite colors?" will talk with Mom in a positive afterglow. The honest response helped a child feel good about his effort.

— 〉 〉 〉 —————————————————

Insulating kids is all about boosting self-esteem. When a school says, "Let's do everything we can to help kids feel good about themselves," the kids feel free to turn in poor quality work, because they know they can redo their work five, six, seven times. That's doing kids a disservice. We're helping them feel good about mediocrity. Kids are so capable, but we expect so little from them.

Betsy, mother of three

2. Encourage self-reliant behavior. For example, children should learn how to manage time, including situations when they complain, "I'm bored." Children who are accustomed to living by parent-determined schedules might need suggestions before becoming totally self-reliant or able to make their own decisions. If you help a child transition from insulation to self-reliance, you might say, "We have 15 minutes before supper. You can swing in the backyard, brush the cat, or help me carry in the groceries. Your choice." After this scenario is repeated several times, a parent can step back and let the child determine how to use the downtime. By then, the child should have the confidence to think for himself.

3. Help your child feel special. When giving compliments, focus on unique traits, skills, or abilities. God has given your child special talents. Highlight those gifts with sincere and specific comments.

In our risk-aware society, we must protect our children. However, if we isolate them from problems and issues, they won't know how to react when we're not around. For example, after a poor recital performance, instead of saying to a child, "Forget it," apply the "learn, grow, and go"

>>>

We visited a school to see if it was what we wanted for our children. When we walked down the hallway, the kindergarten art looked like it had been done by Picasso. We wouldn't choose a school where the art—and who knows what else— was done by the parents, which was the case at this school.

Kimberly, mother of four

formula: Learn the appropriate lessons from the experience, grow stronger and wiser from it, then go on with life.

After your daughter has recovered from the initial disappointment of a poor performance, review how she practiced for the recital. Discuss how she felt before and afterward. Talk about what she might do differently next time in terms of preparation or controlling her nerves. As a result, this "poor" performance might be the most valuable in her career.

Or, instead of doing your son's chores because he's tired, suggest he go to bed early and get up early to finish. Next time, he might use his time more wisely.

Insulation is for houses, not children.

13

KAGOY

> What does it mean?

KAGOY is the acronym for a social phenomenon known as "Kids Are Growing Older Younger"; also referred to as "age compression."

> Why should I care?

This artificial "skewing upward" affects a child's choice of playthings, décor, clothing, hairstyle, and leisure activities. For example, your seven year old might complain, "Toys are for kids," even though your older son played with the identical action figures until his tenth birthday. This is because the timeframe has shrunk in which children play with traditional toys, including all-time favorite baby dolls and toy cars. So many playthings have been down-aged that KAGOY has been labeled "the scourge of the toy industry." Age compression has triggered such a major shift that the Toy Industry Association lowered the definition of childhood from ages 0–14 to 0–10. They now consider preschool as ages 0–2. [1]

However, some of the most obvious signs of KAGOY are seen among older kids. The lines have blurred between tweens (8 to 12 year olds) and teens (13 to 19 year olds.) One example is teen magazines: They are devoured by tween girls. And while girls giggle over the newest fads and fashions, preadolescent boys tune into music with lyrics targeted for more mature listeners.

Age compression often becomes visible in what a child does when a friend is around when compared to how a child acts when he's with family. Of course, children have always shown a public and private face; showing off in front of peers is not new. But extreme behavior among KAGOY-influenced children casts a darker shadow because of the easy availability of alcohol, drugs, and weapons.

KAGOY can trick us into thinking developmental needs have changed. They haven't. Children are not skipping developmental stages, but the outward signs make it appear that children are growing older at a younger age.

> *What can I do?*

Don't be misled by a child's pseudosophistication. We might assume that because a six year old wears glittery eye shadow for the dance recital, she isn't afraid of the dark. Or, because an eight year old can fix a computer glitch, he doesn't worry about coming home to an empty house after school. Children are only embracing the artificial indicators—including clothes and accessories—that they are older than their chronological age.

Children and their parents differ most often on issues of style, not substance. This implies that you and your child might have different standards for length of pants or number of earrings. However, you might agree on issues of faith or alcohol use. Don't let KAGOY-influenced style concerns drain emotional energy and overshadow the more important issues.

How can you learn what a six year old is actually like without being tricked by this up-aging? Refer to reputable sources for information on human development. Many pediatric practices distribute lists of Web sites with reliable information. Most medical doctors offer developmental guidelines during regular checkups. Parenting magazines have excellent sections that focus on developmental levels. Clip those sections and keep them in a notebook for handy reference. Often, additional background is freely available on the corresponding periodical Web sites. Over the course of a calendar year, most major milestones for

> > >

After a girl grows out of size seven, the clothes start looking like "tiny teen" wear. Every year, I hear parents complain that clothes for girls are so inappropriate. I realize it's easier to go into a store and buy what's there, but for us, it's worth the extra effort to shop around and find something that is not geared toward the "tiny teen" look. I have a nine-year-old daughter, and she needs clothes that match her age.

Lesley, mother of four

each level of childhood will be addressed in those publications. Or, insert a child's age into your Internet search engine and scan information from reputable sources including universities, associations, or national professional groups.

Regardless of the KAGOY-influenced behaviors your child adopts, you can be certain that God's timeline for your child's growth is perfect.

14

Kidad Clutter

》 What is it?

The blitz of commercial messages that reach children.

》 Why should I care?

The ad wave is both extensive and intensive as children are aggressively courted as consumers. Commercial messages on strollers are mobile billboards, toys in children's fast-food meals promote television characters, and tweens watch mini ads on cell phone screens. Even paying for a movie ticket doesn't buy freedom from ads anymore. Advertising surrounds us and our children.

Some marketing messages are beneficial. Ads have traditionally been excellent sources of information. Through advertising, a child learns about products even before he learns to read. Internet kidads have made product knowledge readily accessible. Instead of going from store to store, a dad and his daughter can sit side by side then click to learn about toy features and their availability. This is especially useful when children include "must-have" toys on wish lists.

Corporate marketers have written a kidad map to reach your child wherever he is. That's why a 12 year old who is an active blogger on a motion picture site might receive a prerelease movie poster. The company can count on him to do P2P (peer to peer) marketing for the film. The roadmap also reaches a six year old who counts smiling pitchers of a juice drink when she plays an online game and a three year old who requests a specific cereal because she likes the mascot. This down-aging isn't surprising, as even toddlers have brand preferences. As a result, kidad clutter is like surround sound—impossible to escape.

However, there are reasons for concern. The sheer number of kidads signals the potentially early onset of materialism. Overexposure to kidad clutter may lead a child to prefer things to people, or place a higher value on a new toy than time with Grandma.

⟩ What can I do?

Be alert to the multiple touchpoints between advertisers and your child. For example, "advergames" integrate advertisements into Internet video games. Kids play online games against a backdrop of company logos; products become counters and players. You might note that this form of suggestive selling works. If a child plays with online candy, soon he might want to sample the real thing. A major entertainment company recently took advergaming a step further: Children who earn virtual points can redeem their winnings for T-shirts and other tangible prizes when visiting the company theme park.

View kidads within a developmental framework. Younger children haven't developed the mental skills to separate truth from "spin." Because they are concrete thinkers, five and six year olds tend to believe what they see. Ads and content merge together; a child doesn't separate them. By about the age of eight, a child will understand that a book in a cereal box can be another form of advertising. Until then, a child will simply absorb kidads.

When shopping with a concrete thinker, help the child focus on what he can see and feel. Show your child where to look for the number of popsicles in a box, or to compare the weight on two brands of peanut butter. Keep comparisons simple and real.

Kidads targeted to four to seven year olds represent a major shift in marketing. In the past, most advertising messages for "big kids" (older than preschoolers but not yet tweens) came through you, the gatekeeper. But today, kidads might skip you and directly target your child. For

> 〉〉〉
>
> *It's no wonder that product placement in kids' movies has exploded—it works! I remember that my son was a little guy when E.T. first came out, a film in which Reese's Pieces candy was featured prominently. For the next few weeks after he saw that, you can guess what my boy wanted every time we went to the store.*
>
> Brian, father of two

example, an ad five years ago might have highlighted the nutritional content of a sport drink for high parent appeal. A kidad might focus on taste or making independent choices, two elements important to "big kids."

Tweens understand the purpose of advertising. However, 8 to 12 year olds don't always catch the subtle messages of suggestive selling. For example, a 10 year old might want a certain backpack, not because it's such a great product, but because he likes the laser lock he saw advertised. Guide your child to look beyond the kidad. You might say, "This bigger backpack is exactly the same without the lock. What if all your books don't fit into the smaller pack? Do you want to carry notebooks separately?"

Look for signs of kidad clutter when you grocery shop. Cereal with toy premiums may be shelved lower, at your child's eye level. Floor ads, which are closer to children than adults, are usually in departments with high kid appeal, like snacks and beverages.

What's the bottom line on kidads? Some provide valuable information. Others provide teaching opportunities. One thing is certain: With the popularity of technology and the growing market savvy of children, kidad clutter will only become more appealing.

>>> 15

Kidfluence+

> What is it?

An indicator of children's rank and power in a family.

> Why should I care?

Generations of parents have dealt with the "nag factor" or "pester power." But the sphere of children's influence now extends beyond the grocery-store candy aisle. Kidfluence has become kid power. Here's the new equation: children + tech talents + money = kidfluence plus.

Children have a high degree of comfort with technology. They've grown up in a digital age. Unlike their parents, perhaps, children aren't afraid the computer will melt if they hit the wrong key. Their tech confidence has contributed to a noticeable skewing in the family hierarchy. Parents sometimes unconsciously fuel this sense of empowerment. For example, in past years when something technical went wrong, the classic solution was, "Wait until Dad comes home." Today, if the DVD doesn't work properly, Dad might ask his 10 year old, "Can you fix this thing?"

This tech-triggered power shift has deepened with money. Children today are richer than children of previous generations. Even young children have money, and all ages spend money. This combination of knowledge and money combine to create kidfluence+.

As a result, children are being directly targeted as consumers; after all, companies prefer customers who are rich and smart. Children have assumed two distinct roles in the marketplace: Kids themselves are buyers, and they are major influencers for adult purchases.

Marketers know this is happening. They know a child may pressure you into an unplanned purchase when you enter an elaborately themed environment, see attention-getting displays, participate in product

› › ›

When my son was about 14, we took a family vacation to Yellowstone National Park. We chose the destination in part because Kent Jr. was really into drawing at the time. And when we got to the Grand Canyon of the Yellowstone at Artist Point, he was so fascinated by the falls that we stayed there for several hours while he made a good start on a landscape. My wife even held an umbrella over him and his sketchbook for half an hour in a light rain!

Kent, father of one

demonstrations, and attend events. As a result, some parents feel a sense of helplessness when trying to combat a child's persuasive abilities.

Kidfluence+ is more than nagging for an ice-cream cone. Children today determine where to pick up supper and where to spend summer vacation. Years ago, parents were the sole decision-makers. Today, buying decisions are characterized by an ongoing dialogue between parent and child.

❭ What can I do?

Model decision-making as related to purchasing. If the grocery store has a sale on canned vegetables, say, "Please put five cans of corn in the cart. I buy canned goods when they are on sale." Your child will observe that wise buying begins with logical thinking, not an advertisement or promotion. Monetary rewards can reinforce positive messages for today's fiscally-aware kids. Teach your child at an early age how to clip and organize grocery coupons. Then when you shop together, let him keep half the money you save. Some parents even encourage children to print coupons from the Internet.

Be alert to your own shopping personality. For example, are you an impulse shopper? If so, think through how you handled your child's most recent request at the checkout line. How will you respond next time? Advance preparation for a plan of action can avoid your child's meltdown and your overspending.

Don't be afraid to veto a child's choice or disagree with his suggestions. You are still the market gatekeeper. If you want your child to participate in a purchase decision, your child can choose within the guidelines you set.

For example, you might say, "We have money for one day at the theme park or two days at a museum and zoo. Which do you prefer?"

Your child may be an expert in some areas. That's the reason some parents defer to children when making choices in fashion, music, entertainment, or technology. Some parents ask their children to research household products or services. For example, when buying a new cell phone, a 12 year old may know more than you do about the features to look for and the pitfalls of sign-up plans. Decide in which areas you trust your child's judgment.

Kidfluence+ can be an actual plus. Parents who seek quality time with their children can involve them in collaborative decision-making. When a parent and child discuss options that will affect the family, they both work toward the family good. Children bring their personal perspective to decisions. When they see that their opinions are valued, they learn the value of respect. When they participate in discussions with multiple viewpoints, children learn to compromise. Parents who are alert to the potential of kidfluence+ can channel this trend to benefit their family.

〉〉〉 16

Luxe Kids

〉 *What is it?*

The result of parents who "trade up" for their children.

〉 *Why should I care?*

Generations of parents have felt that "nothing is too good for my child."
Until now, that sentiment was realized only by affluent parents. Today,
social factors have combined so that trading up to luxury is not limited
to the wealthy. Women and children influence more spending than in
previous generations. More highly educated parents and older parents
have more disposable income.

In addition, we have experienced a steady increase in the standard of
living. Luxury products have also gone mainstream. Upscale diaper bags
are sold where Mom shops for budget detergent. Internationally famous

designers have discovered the lucrative, middle-class children's market and are creating mass-market versions of boutique product lines. Class distinction is blurred when tweens wear designer labels to walk the dog.

Parents and grandparents who wear name brands are delighted to outfit children in similar styles. The designers are even happier, for they have an opportunity to develop brand loyalty beginning in infancy. Cynics comment that children have become a commodity. And, of course, parents who favor luxury brands for themselves can expect their kids to adopt the same attitude.

However, some of the spending is a reflection of the times in which we live. Everyday treats might emotionally balance the concern parents feel about raising children in the shadow of ever-present world conflict and worry about homeland security. Some parents pamper children to compensate for spending long hours at the office. Parents who travel on business attempt to buy favors with expensive gifts when they miss a child's recital or big game.

Along with living in a nice neighborhood and driving a nice car, some parents now make a well-dressed child a priority. The type of stroller—umbrella, travel system, all-terrain, or jogger—becomes an extension of an upscale lifestyle. The type of entertainment at a child's birthday party—pony rides, a clown, or a magician—buys status in the neighborhood. Affordability has driven purchases, as many premier brand products can be cloned and offered at a lower price than the original. However, many parents must still trade down—cut the costs somewhere else—in order to trade up.

But luxury *experiences* can't be easily duplicated. As a result, premier experiences are still an exclusive option for parents with deep pockets. At some spas, three year olds can sign up for "My First Manicure," "My First Facial," or "My First Pedicure." Although the emotional benefits and the sense of indulgence may justify the cost, parents must answer the question, "Are these experiences appropriate for children?"

〉 What can I do?

Luxe kids often assume *"I want"* means *"I get."* This expectation might be for something as inexpensive as a candy bar or as costly as the newest tech toy. If your child has this expectation, re-examine what you are communicating about money. Don't be afraid to say no when asked about a purchase. If your child is above the age of eight, when logical thought patterns begin to develop, briefly explain the reason behind your non-buying decision. Avoid extended discussions; simply share your rationale and move on.

Luxe kids may have the mistaken notion that money buys happiness. One of the most effective ways to correct this perception is family participation in a worthwhile cause. For example, you might start jar jingles.

〉〉〉

My seven year old was best friends with a little girl who visited Hawaii with her parents. That evening, I asked him how his friend's trip had been. My son was full of information. Then he asked when we were taking him to Hawaii. I said, "When you're old enough to pay for the trip yourself."

Sue, mother of three

Simply set a jar on the kitchen counter. When anyone enters with loose change, the coins get dropped into the jar. When the container is heavy, the children count the change and donate it to a worthy cause. In the process, parents can emphasize the underlying concept that giving to others brings joy.

Children might consider donating their hair to other children with medical hair loss (www.locksoflove.org). Families can learn about visiting hospitals and nursing homes with their pets (www.deltasociety.org) or serving as puppy raisers for guide dogs (www.guidedogsofAmerica.org). These giving actions can help luxe kids put money, possessions, and social status into a more balanced perspective.

There is nothing wrong with the luxurious feeling that comes from wearing a quality coat or enjoying dinner at a special restaurant. But when luxury becomes an expectation, or when the question "Is that all?" is often asked, it's time to ask, "Am I raising a luxe child?"

〉〉〉 17

Magic Money

〉 *What is it?*

Credit/debit cards for children and teens.

〉 *Why should I care?*

How times change. Ten years ago, parents asked their friends, "Will your son have a credit card at college?" Five years ago, parents asked, "Does your teenager have a credit card?" Now parents ask, "Does your fifth grader have a credit card?"

The drop-down credit-card issue isn't surprising. Because of kid-fluence+, even six and seven year olds are accustomed to handling and spending money. Our children, who belong to the "instant gratification generation," naturally covet personal plastic because it's so fast and convenient.

But is it wise?

Representatives of credit card companies are quick to note three advantages:

1. Children who use credit cards while they still live at home will have supervision during the learning process and then know how to use credit responsibly when they are older.

2. Kid cards are flexible. Children can make purchases or get money out of an ATM.

3. Kid cards help parents and children track purchases online.

But parents and educators are also quick to point out that, contrary to messages children may receive, there is no free money. Even after the age of eight, when children become more abstract thinkers, the common thinking is, *With a credit card, I can get anything.* This false assumption

---

⟩ ⟩ ⟩

My husband gave each of our teens a credit card (on the family account) when they got their driver's licenses. In return, they were expected to occasionally shop for the family, run errands, purchase gas, and keep track of their personal spending. At the end of each month, my husband went over the bill with each teen. Our kids learned to comparison shop and manage their money, and we as parents benefited by having help with the shopping and errands. Today our kids are in high school, college, and graduate school, and all are excellent money managers.

Kathy, mother of three

also attracts some adults. Buying transactions are more "real" to kids when they hand over the actual cash.

Many children walk around with loaded pockets. They carry store loyalty cards, gift cards, and now plastic cash. The phrase "credit cards with training wheels" describes cards that are branded with the image of a popular celebrity or movie license. These cards target children as young as the age of eight. Unfortunately, these kids may learn some tough lessons before realizing that magic money is neither free nor limitless.

⟩ What can I do?

Find out when your child's school begins to teach financial literacy. Also ask if the curriculum is from a financial institution, credit-card company, math textbook, or consumer advocacy group. The source of the material may slant the perspective of what your child learns (see "Undercover Advertising"). Because money cards are so readily available to even young children, lessons about credit typically begin in middle school.

Parents at home are following the same timeline. This is wise, because until legislation bans the sale of personal information of minors, children may innocently provide contact information that is used by credit-card companies. Many parents will not permit children to complete contest forms or warranty cards. The personal information (name, address, phone, birthday) children give on Web sites, chat rooms, or online bulletin boards can trigger a deluge of applications for "fun ways to shop" (i.e. credit cards).

Ultimately, many parents conclude that their children really don't need a credit card before the teen years. And even then, parents need to assess whether a particular teen is ready for the responsibility that goes with the privilege. To determine this, some parents apply the cell phone test. The parent might say, "After you purchase and successfully manage paying for a cell phone for six months, then we can talk about the possibility of a credit card." Other parents require a teen to save for a long-term purchase, plus demonstrate wise buying practices, before permitting plastic money.

If and when your teen is ready for a credit card, examine options together. A prepaid card, in which a parent transfers money into an account and the teen spends it down, offers a built-in safeguard: Parents can limit the amount their child is spending. Another option is debit cards that impose limits. Or linked debit cards that can be used for specific purchases. Some credit cards offer plans with card limits customized for each family member. Other parents choose to co-sign a credit card for their teen.

Too many teens still view plastic money as free money, not a plastic loan. Make sure your teen understands how credit and interest work. Use an online calculator to demonstrate how long it takes to pay off a high interest credit card bill.

PC immersion (see page 87) communicates to children that a credit card, like a cell phone, is a necessity. Whenever you allow these and other products to enter your child's life, the teaching you do and the limits you set will help your child make mature decisions about their use.

Mousers

> *What is it?*

Infants and toddlers who use lapware (software for pre-readers).

> *Why should I care?*

Software for babies and toddlers is designed to be used with an adult, which explains the term "lapware." The phenomenon of dot-com babies begins at the age of six months, or about the same time a child can sit upright without a wobbly head.

Lapware is designed to introduce a very young child to the keyboard, mouse, and screen. Many products build on the concept of "baby bang": A mouser randomly hits the keyboard, then watches something happen on the screen or hears something through the computer speakers.

Lapware developers intentionally include tech elements that let a cyber-tot feel good about what he's done or have a sense of achievement. This can contribute to growing a healthy self-concept. A social component is built into lapware by requiring an adult to participate, at least during the initial months of use. This fits into the parental desire for bonding. Product marketers emphasize that lapware can enhance learning potential at an early age, which is appropriate for babies growing up in the Information Age. Most lapware can be customized by the parent to include photos of pets, voices of family members, and length of time a game will continue.

A mouser can look impressive. Parents are sometimes amazed that a two year old can point and click on a computer before he knows how to share a toy with another child. However, early childhood educators might ask, "What's wrong with this picture?"

Many professionals who work with young children question potential benefits and note possible negatives of lapware. Research shows that very young children learn more from real objects than pictures of objects. For example, a toddler learns more about a flower by touching the stem and sniffing the petals than by seeing a picture of a flower.

A young child may be fascinated by technology, but does he learn from it? That's one of many unanswered questions. Clinicians are just now on the front end of long-term study. Researchers must also address questions that already nag parents of young children, including: Do mousers have shorter attention spans? Do mousers and non-mousers show similar levels of creativity? How does repeated use of lapware affect brain development? Can mousers avoid repetitive stress injuries?

Although the questions continue, we know that lapware is becoming increasingly attractive. Unfortunately, today's babies will be teens by the time we have the answers to guide us. Until that time, we need to go beyond "cute" and "fun" when assessing the potential value of lapware and the impact on would-be mousers.

〉 What can I do?

While researchers are busy with clinical studies, parents should ask their own questions before buying lapware. Start with these:

Why should my baby be a mouser?

How will my child benefit from sitting at the computer?

What would my baby be doing if he weren't plugged in?

Does lapware offer meaningful experiences my baby can't get elsewhere?

Educators are concerned that lapware will become the caregiver for a generation of mousers. After all, we've already seen electronic babysitters emerge among toddlers who watch videos and television. Whether or not your child becomes a PC-tyke, lapware should never substitute for building with blocks or splashing in the tub. Children's needs are met by being mentally and physically active through these activities.

Based on current information, many developmentalists feel babies

〉〉〉

Children learn about computers early on. My three year old looked at my husband's wireless mouse and asked, "How come Daddy's doesn't have a rope?"

Kimberly, mother of four

should not be wired until after the age of three; this is when they can connect their action with the mouse to what they see on the screen. Parents know that three year olds also follow directions (at least sometimes), but inappropriate content must still be blocked on the computer.

A lapware label does not certify that the content is appropriate for your child. For example, some simple racing games for young children contain elements of violence, such as shooting a weapon. Lapware requires the same vigilant parental monitoring as any other type of media.

Carefully consider issues on both sides of the debate before your child becomes a mouser. Stay alert as research is released. Just because a two year old can insert a CD-ROM into a computer does not mean that's what your child should be doing.

>>> 19

Organic Mom

> What is it?

A mother whose awareness of body, mind, and spirit issues shapes her lifestyle.

> Why should I care?

Today's new-style mom mentally compartmentalizes tasks to organize her day but is driven by a search for balance among lifestyle segments. Equilibrium is possible because the organic mom is fluent in technology, multitasks effectively, and sees through cultural clutter to focus on what's authentic. Children are a priority, but not the only priority—she and her husband matter too. She places a high value on time. Although today's "mom market" is segmented into mini-niches, mothers are similar in their organically integrated approach to life.

Front-cover stories note the body-mind-spirit connection. Mom-targeted Web sites and blogs include content to increase physical, mental, and social well-being. Whether it's a bag of snack food or a body wash, product packaging reflects a three-pronged "good for you" emphasis. Marketers are aware that organic moms know what contributes to living right.

A family meal is a typical example of this organic thinking. Research shows that families who eat together eat more healthfully.[1] Sharing a meal of "good food that's good for you," talking about what happened at school and in news headlines, and saying a mealtime prayer offer premium quality time. What children put into their bodies, minds, and souls at the dinner table matters to the organic mom.

Although some observers dismiss this as merely "feel-good" parenting, it's more than that. The organic mom intentionally focuses on the triple elements that contribute to healthy living. That's why organic moms take a proactive, not reactive, approach to lifestyle issues. For example, they monitor their children's activities and participate in family fitness. They teach portion control at meals and offer healthy food choices. These parents also prioritize character development and want children to have a spiritual foundation. As a result, organic moms make wise decisions that they anticipate will last a lifetime.

> ### What can I do?

Consider how mind-body-spirit thinking influences you. Some organic moms view themselves as lifestyle managers for their children. The mental triangle provides a structure that makes it easy to see if something tips out of balance. If an area shifts in an unhealthy direction, focus on a single area and make one change at a time. But as all parents know, actual or long-term change often requires more than merely adult effort. When changes require a child's participation, such as taking water instead of soda to a baseball game or eating granola snacks instead of candy bars, give lots of positive reinforcement.

Retail is starting to cater to the organic mom. Some grocery stores play classical music and offer massage chairs alongside the sushi bar. Look for ways these new options can boost the wellness level of your family. As one commentator noted, stores aren't just selling food today, they're selling life.[2] And it's healthy life, because even the youngest shoppers are alert to healthy-living issues.

— 〉〉〉 ——————————————

My daughter scooped out a satellite-dish-sized serving of ice cream. "That's the largest half-cup serving I've ever seen," I said, sneaking up behind her.

"But I'm so hungry after soccer practice!"

"If your body is that hungry, what does it probably need?"

"More protein. More minerals." She knows the drill. That was two months ago. Yesterday she came home from a class party. "Mom," she said, "you've ruined me. I could only eat one cookie and drink half a can of Sprite. Too much sugar makes me sick now."

Those were some of the sweetest words I've ever heard!

Marianne, mother of three

In schools, the mind-body-spirit focus is evident in the shift toward teaching wellness as a lifestyle. Stress-reduction techniques are often taught before children take standardized tests. In cafeterias, pop vending machines are being replaced with black-and-white "cow" milk machines. Physical education is becoming more than merely a time to change clothes and take attendance. Find out what your child's school is doing. Make time for family fitness. The most effective example for healthy living begins at home. Take bike rides together after dinner or walk through the park. These types of activities can initiate conversation and are a good alternative to watching TV or punching keys on a computer game. Children that see Mom and Dad exercising absorb important messages about self-respect and self-discipline.[3]

Organic moms typically find ways to integrate elements of wellness into everyday life: Children don't notice when she adds oatmeal to the meatloaf. Kids will enjoy a family game of hopscotch, perhaps unaware that they are exercising and improving coordination skills. Volunteering as a family to help clean the park provides an opportunity to work together while instilling environment-friendly lessons.

The organic style of parenting is driven by developing positive habits early. Keeping fruits and veggies around the house provides easy access to healthy snacks. Taking time as a family to serve meals at a soup kitchen teaches children that they can make a difference in their community. A six year old will assume that you always buy an extra Thanksgiving turkey for the school food drive. But that's the type of attention to soul food that makes a lifelong impact on a child.

20

Pay2play

> ## > What is it?

Students are charged fees for participation in school activities.

> ## > Why should I care?

The budget crunch in education initially triggered the pay2play phenomenon. Lack of money continues to fuel the controversy. As school activity budgets shrink, students are being asked to fund their participation. Although pay2play sports have received the greatest attention, students are also being charged participation fees for music, drama, and even service organizations such as student council. This is happening at elementary, middle, and high-school levels in suburban, rural, and urban schools in states that do not ban assessing fees for public school students.

Pay2play charges are sometimes called stealth fees because "uniform rental" or "transportation charge" camouflages the fact that to play, a child must pay. Some schools request that parents "donate" a specific amount. Other schools ask students to raise a minimum amount of money through fund-raising. But school administrators point out that selling magazine subscriptions, candy, and wrapping paper only begins to pay the actual cost of coaches' salaries and officials' stipends. Funding must also be found for field maintenance, uniforms, equipment, and other costs.

Passing tax levies has been minimally successful, as the pay2play issue is emotionally charged. Voters who believe that extracurricular activities are truly "extras" feel that the players should pay for the privilege of playing football. Others believe that increasing ticket prices appropriately charges those who attend the events.

〉〉〉

Pay2play started early in our family's education experience. Starting in fourth grade, the school asked parents to pay for "gifted" programming—the district deemed that providing challenging curriculum for high-achieving children was a perk with a price tag. Additionally, in our district the kids who qualify for free lunches are exempt from the extracurricular fees so all kids can participate—in theory. But parents still have to arrange rides to and from practice and games plus purchase the right personal equipment, and some moms and dads don't have the resources to accomplish that.

Mary, mother of three

Even if students can afford the costs, pay2play generates other issues. For example, parents may assume that paying a fee guarantees a certain amount of stage time for their thespian or playing time for their basketball player. If each sport department develops specific pay2play policies, there may be inconsistencies in refund procedures. Schools that offer exceptions to students who can't pay create a two-tier system, which can be embarrassing for students and awkward for administrators.

In spite of the concerns, pay2play is a growing trend. Educators note that assessed fees appear to lead to lower levels of student participation. Parents comment on the irony that the childhood obesity crisis has triggered widespread conversation, but now students must pay to be physically active. Other parents are concerned that children who can't afford to pay will have blanks on college applications and be unable to compete for scholarships.

And yet social commentators anticipate that student activities will no longer have a free ride. Today's challenge is to find both short-term and long-term solutions.

❭ What can I do?

If participation fees are creating divisions in your school or community, research how other schools handle the issue. Share that information with other parents, school administrators, businesses, and local government to create alternatives to the current policy.

In addition to soliciting corporate involvement (see "Undercover Advertising"), some schools ask parents to donate their time, not just their money. As a result, some parents coach teams or serve as club sponsors.

Others assume administrative functions and care for equipment, wardrobe, or props. This "active-level" parental involvement can create another set of issues, beginning with implications for the student-parent relationship. Younger children, who are more egocentric than older kids, may find it difficult to share their mom or dad with their peers. Parents, too, might have a hard time switching between Dad and club sponsor. For example, does Coach Dad give his daughter a starting position instead of a more qualified player?

We are on the front end of the pay2play trend. There is currently more talk about the problems than the solutions. Few truly creative approaches to the issue have even been attempted. But unless a new paradigm is developed, in the future a free education may end at the classroom door, not the football field.

21

PC Immersion

〉 *What is it?*

The 24/7 influence of pop culture.

〉 *Why should I care?*

Cultural noise surrounds our children. Although parents have historically complained that the peer group is a strong and sometimes negative influence, peers have major competition today. Heavy doses of music, sports, television, celebrities, video games, movies, and Internet-generated media offer "24-tainment" to children. As a result, parents, especially those with tweens and teens, feel they face a fierce battle against outside influences.

Developmentally, a child's search for identity strengthens and focuses during preadolescence. One of the ways 8 to 19 year olds distinguish themselves is by discovering and then latching onto people, issues, even foods that the culture defines as "cool" at the moment. These and other elements combine to shape their unique generational personality.

Historically, tweens and teens have teetered at the furthest edge of cool. This has been obvious in fashion, music, entertainment, and other lifestyle choices. As each generation of children moves into adolescence, they embrace what feels right for them. After all, this is their time in history. As a result, some parents feel shut out as they watch their almost-grown children drift into the world of pop culture.

Not all elements of today's PC immersion are negative. Celebrities and sports stars draw attention to social issues and worthy causes. Regardless of where children live, they are growing up ethnic aware and color blind. They are tolerant of differences among people. Although this acceptance can go too far, the generational personality that is emerging today has a worldwide perspective. But current cultural noise is significantly different from that of the past.

Today's PC immersion is potentially dangerous. The violent themes in media desensitize viewers. Sexual immorality is a recurring theme in

>)))

PC immersion shows itself in different ways. I've noticed a self-reliant attitude developing in younger children today. Kids want to emulate what they see and hear in movies and on television. Kids are so visual today. They see so much at such young ages.

Emily, mother of three

socially irresponsible entertainment. These are especially critical concerns for children and youth, who are vulnerable to outside influences while they develop a framework for personal views and values they will hold forever.

〉 What can I do?

Stay connected. Appearing "too cool" for the family is only a youthful cover-up. Kids, even tweens and teens, care about what parents think. Use sports, music, movies, or other relevant topics to launch new levels of connectedness with your child. Learn by listening. Grow by observing.

Develop new touchpoints with your child. As children age, their interests mature. Their skills of observation deepen. Their attention becomes more focused. Is your six year old ready to attend a matinee performance of live theater? Is your 10 year old now ready to attend a symphony concert? These can be new touchpoints. Be honest with your child when he crosses a threshold of appropriateness. Then instruct by influencing and modeling, not lecturing.

Parents and older kids often link through parallel activities. Shovel the driveway with your child, clean out a closet together, or even sort coupons side by side. Find comfortable times to talk together. Discussing a recent movie or headline issue is less threatening when you and your child work as partners and conversation evolves naturally.

Spending time together is critical. Your child is inundated by pop culture at every turn. Media teach. Entertainment informs. The Internet influences. You can and should teach, inform, and influence, too. However, that can only happen if you and your child intersect frequently.

Kids are on a continual hunt for the coolest and newest. Those two elements drive pop culture. But today's kids care about their families, too. They want to spend time doing family activities. Despite what your kids may tell you, they really are interested in knowing what parents think and believe. Beneath the sheen of "cool" and "new" pop culture, children still absorb family influences.

22

Playpen Sports

> What is it?

The umbrella term for organized sports targeted to toddlers and preschoolers.

> Why should I care?

Two year olds now toddle onto tennis courts with rackets. Three year olds drag bats to baseball diamonds, and four year olds practice teeing off at the golf course. This is a reflection of KAGOY.

Some observers view this downward creep as a natural reflection of our sports-crazed society. Others view playpen sports as a viable alternative to young children sitting in front of screens. In a somewhat ironic twist, videos introduce babies to sport fundamentals. For example, phrases such as "Hit the baseball" and "Catch the baseball" are repeatedly played against a backdrop of baseball scenes.

Even during early childhood, children clearly prefer one activity over another. Some preschoolers may be only marginally interested in kicking a ball or playing catch. However, all children should be exposed to developmentally appropriate activities that build large motor skills.

Optimistic observers hope playpen sports will prevent childhood obesity and result in a lifelong love of physical activity. But rushing the net can backfire: Down-aging organized sports may contribute to the burnout increasingly observed among middle schoolers.

〉 What can I do?

A baby or toddler does not need to participate in organized sports to develop age-appropriate motor skills. Avoid falling into the playpen sports trap by joining your child in these sample activities that reflect a developmental timeline:

Before the age of two:

- Children can kneel without support. Some toddlers kneel with legs flayed apart to the sides. Encourage floor-based play with blocks and vehicles a child can move back and forth.
- Children can pull wheeled toys; push toddler-sized wagons. Rotate toys regularly, so that everything is not visible at the same time. When you reintroduce a wheel toy several weeks later, a toddler will be at a different level of development and may use the toy in a totally new way.

Two year old:
- Children can walk alone. Play a backyard game of "chase."
- Children can walk up and down stairs. (Twos typically do not alternate feet on stairs. Some twos may need some assistance, especially on an unfamiliar or long staircase.) Provide opportunities to practice climbing stairs, especially if you live in a single floor home.
- Children can toss a ball underhand. Play catch with a fairly large, pliable ball.
- Child can bend over and right himself without toppling over. A child can pick up toys on the floor.

Three year old:
- Children can walk on tiptoe. Build "tiptoe to bed" into the nap and nighttime routines.

I was in a local coffee shop the other day when in walked a group of nine three year olds wearing the littlest green soccer uniforms I'd ever seen. They all piled into a corner booth as the "coach" took one of the tiny members to the counter and ordered five frozen mocha drinks. I have no idea if those kids' parents knew their little powerhouses were being rewarded with caffeinated sugar shots, but I didn't have to wonder where all their aggressive energy was from.

Mick, father of two

- Children can jump with feet together. Play "jump over the cracks" on concrete sidewalks.
- Children can kick a large ball (without direction) and extend their arms to catch a bounced ball. Use the same type of large, flexible ball for catching and kicking.

Four year old:

- Children can hop on one foot. Use sidewalk chalk to mark hopscotch.
- Children can run with a clear sense of direction and the ability to start and stop. Set up a backyard obstacle course using buckets and garbage pails.
- Children can walk forward on a straight line. Chalk a line on the driveway and play "Don't fall off the high wire."
- Children can throw overhand. Play catch using a smaller ball that feels comfortable to child. Gradually increase distance from child.

Unspoken questions frequently float around playpen sports venues. Well-intentioned parents wonder, *Will attending a golf clinic at the age of three help my child beat the competition at the age of four or five?* Or, *Does participating in a sports clinic position my two year old for a college scholarship?* Addressing these concerns isn't nearly as important as this fundamental question: *What is best for my child?*

〉〉〉 23

Ratings Creep

〉 What is it?

The sometimes-subtle shift of media and entertainment ratings that allows increasing amounts of profanity, violence, and sexual situations.

〉 Why should I care?

Movies, video games, television programs, and other forms of media are ranked by imposed and voluntary standards. Ratings can trigger heated debate among legislators, lobbyists, parents, and children. This is especially evident immediately after a high-profile incident with a strong "cringe factor."

When surveyed, parents often want stronger regulations. However, even when tighter controls are imposed, moms and dads emerge at various points on the ratings continuum. Some parents do not use ratings.

Others don't understand them or ignore them. Still others rely heavily on ratings to determine what is appropriate for their children. And in the meantime, the definition of content suitable for various ages continues to shift.

A special challenge comes from new media: Parents often don't understand it, but their children do. Enforcing limits or censoring content in such situations can quickly become an exercise in futility with a high level of frustration.

Ratings across media categories are neither consistent nor consistently accurate. Because ratings do not always reflect content, viewers can be exposed to unexpected images, language, or situations. As a result, confidence in ratings has eroded among some media users.

And yet children are surrounded by technology. They are media savvy. They are drawn to emerging forms of entertainment. They are early and fast adopters of new technology. Can parents trust ratings to help monitor what their children see and hear?

⟩ What can I do?

Use ratings as an initial guide or viewing tool. Ratings are a starting point, not the final answer. Even entertainment ratings that match your child's age may contain language or scenes you feel are inappropriate. Apply your personal sensitivity screen within the framework of printed ratings before giving your own stamp of approval. For example, some parents draw strict boundaries with live action media but are more lenient with animated movies or games. Determining appropriateness is not easy; even governmental agencies have had trouble setting standards of acceptability. [1]

Always consider your child's personality and individual traits when judging appropriateness. For example, a scary scene might frighten a sensitive child even in a G-rated movie that's supposedly suitable for family viewing. Age is another variable. Some parents enforce family-wide viewing guidelines. But just as some parents allow older children to stay up later at night than younger children, others set broader media limits for older children. There isn't a single correct way to approach this issue, as different guidelines work for different families.

Recognize that tolerance levels for language, violence, and sexual situations will vary among friends and families. Censorship lines vary even between a mom and dad in the same household. Some parents allow children and youth a significant amount of freedom to self-monitor. Other parents strictly define acceptable content for older children, yet ease the standards when younger children grow up. This often happens when there is a "drop-down" factor: Younger siblings may be exposed to more mature entertainment simply because it is being played or viewed by older brothers or sisters.

With a decade age difference between my two youngest daughters, I've seen the reliability of media ratings decline over the years. Whereas I used to trust cartoons and children's programs when my older daughters were small, I now feel I have to continually monitor the media in our home to avoid exposure to crude jokes, liberal agendas, and sensual messages.

Blanca, mother of three

Although schools include an introduction to media literacy in curriculum, parents have the ultimate responsibility in determining what is acceptable for *their* family. Some parents find that movie and game reviews provide valuable information. Weblogs or parent-driven sites may offer more helpful input than general reviews simply because the reviewer writes from a parental perspective.

Take advantage of resources like *Plugged In*, *Movie Nights*, and *Movie Nights for Kids* by Focus on the Family. These products offer parents valuable insight to possible objectionable content in media, and they also give suggestions for conversation starters and teachable moments. Check out the *Plugged In* Web site (www.pluggedinonline.com) for popular music and movie reviews.

Although published comments may be helpful during the initial screening stage, they also provide excellent "talking points" for parents and children after co-viewing, or watching media together. For example, a parent and child may play a video game, then read a Web-based review and discuss whether the reviewer judged correctly.

When parent and child react to content generated by a neutral third party, responses are channeled toward the content and virtual reviewer, not the family members. This process of watching media and *then* reading a review can be an effective tool to help a child learn to judge appropriateness. Post-viewing discussions triggered by reviews are especially valuable during the tween years when children's responses might be influenced by hormonal swings or flashes of independence unaccompanied by logic. Most media and entertainment commentary will reflect at least some reviewer bias, so be selective.

In sanitized versions of explicit media, offensive words are bleeped out or replaced. These edited copies may be rated differently from original releases. Often, they are even shelved in a different area of the store. However, even these cuts can contain material you might judge inappropriate; although specific words may be deleted, the subject matter is unabridged. As in all situations, use ratings only as a guide.

〉〉〉 24

Rewinders

〉 *What is it?*

Grandparents who provide primary childcare for their grandchildren.

〉 *Why should I care?*

Statistics show that a growing number of grandparents are raising their grandchildren. Although these older adults obviously have previous experience with children, rewinders are typically unprepared for a second round of parenting. Frequently, the need to assume a child's care is immediate.

Grandparents become rewinders for a variety of reasons. Some grandchildren need care because of the death of a parent. Others are children of military parents serving in war zones. But often, the parents are not capable of caring for their children. Research shows that these parents may have substance abuse problems, mental illness, or are incarcerated. As a result of being neglected, abused, or having other problems, the children may have special needs.

Rewinders differ by age, health, ethnicity, background, and religion. Some are embarrassed by the situation. Others are overwhelmed, not only by the physical demands, but also by societal influences that now affect children and youth. Feelings range from, "If I had done a better job the first time around, I wouldn't be a parent again" to "I'm grateful I can help." Some rewinders give short-term care; others are committed to being long-term parents. Some legally adopt their grandchildren. Rewinders typically make large financial and personal sacrifices to provide for the safety and well-being of a second generation of children.

Rewinders face multiple legal issues that may include grandparent rights, guardianship, adoption, powers of attorney, medical consent, and legal custody. Finances are often a major area of concern. Today, there are so many grandparent-headed households that local, state, and national organizations offer a variety of resources. Support groups are sponsored by social service agencies and churches.

> ⟩ ⟩ ⟩

As a teacher, I've worked with all kinds of families. One year I had a student who was living with her grandparents as a result of a tragic accident in her family. Her grandparents never missed a parent-teacher conference or a school program. They were actively involved in her life.

Blanca, mother of three

> *What can I do?*

Parents can be alert to these unique needs of rewinders:

1. Isolation from peers is a problem for grandparents who are parents. Intergenerational groups, seniors clubs, and parental groups should invite rewinders to participate; these people are older adults with younger children, but these "new" parents still have social needs. However, as with other parents, their attendance may depend on the availability of affordable childcare.

2. Be sensitive to the situations rewinders face. Some children call their grandparents Mom and Dad. Other children use more traditional grandparent terminology. When talking with children of rewinders, follow the child's lead in how you refer to the caregivers.

3. Avoid assumptions. Gray hair doesn't mean a rewinder is computer illiterate; gray hair doesn't give a grandpa an innate sense to understand the maze of soccer fields. A rewinder is still a parent; he has lived longer, but each day he faces the joys and challenges that accompany raising a child. A rewinder has additional concerns but deals with the same core issues that face every parent.

> > >

An acquaintance of ours has fathered several children out of wedlock. Since neither he nor the mothers are capable of raising them, emotionally or otherwise, his parents have ended up as surrogate parents to their grandchildren.

Stan, father of one

4. Avoid being critical. Instead, take every opportunity to offer a compliment. Guilt and worry often chip away at a rewinder's confidence in his ability to parent. Your affirmation and acknowledgment will be valued and appreciated.

5. Include rewinders in activities that involve their children. Some grandparents are so physically fit, they might be eager to coach soccer if they can fit it into their busy schedule. Others might not be able to attend an evening auction because of limited night vision, but they would flip pancakes at a Saturday morning breakfast. Don't deny rewinders the opportunity to participate in their children's activities simply because of their advanced age or non-traditional situation. Children of rewinders want to be viewed as "real" families; seeing Grandpa work alongside other parents at a school picnic publicly validates the family.

The phenomenon of grandparents raising grandchildren is not new. However, the increasing number of rewinders presents an emerging social issue that brings together two vulnerable populations: the young and the old. We should remember these families in our prayers and offer support as we are able.

>>> 25

Risk Aware

> What is it?

The post-9/11 heightened state of alertness.

> Why should I care?

Safety is a top priority for parents. Headlines about child abductions and homeland security cast a long, dark shadow. Previous generations of parents were also challenged to protect their children. However, today's parents have an acute awareness that even the latest technology and most advanced law enforcement strategies cannot create a completely risk-free environment. As a result, moms and dads wonder, *How can I equip my child to cope with unknown hazards but not frighten her?*

> *What can I do?*

Begin with simple safety routines. Because kids can count on routines, even simple patterns offer a measure of emotional security. Basic precautions follow a developmentally appropriate timeline, as shown in the following examples:

- Preschooler: "Hold my hand in a parking lot" or "We always stop and look both ways before stepping into the street."
- Five year old: Answer a phone call without giving out family information.
- Seven year old: Ignore an online request for age and address; get parent.
- Nine year old: When home alone, ignore a doorbell or knock on the door; if the door is open or something seems wrong when arriving home, go to the next door neighbor.
- Eleven year old: When in a new situation, stay focused, calm, and aware of surroundings.

As you teach your child to "think smart," remember that children who have been raised in a loving environment are not risk aware; they are naturally trusting. You may need to remind a four year old that it's okay to say no to an adult if the child feels uncomfortable. It's not a sign of weakness to move near the driver if a nine year old is being bullied on the school bus. And you *expect* a 12 year old to go to the camp administrator if a counselor makes an inappropriate advance. Talking about these scenarios, however unlikely, offers both psychological permission and concrete actions for a child to deal with a situation, should it arise.

Fears of young children are fantasy-based, because they cannot separate real from not real. That's the reason a toddler may be afraid to sit near a bathtub drain. An imaginative preschooler may have nightmares about creepy shadows that appear on bedroom walls. Respect these fantasy-based fears; they're very real to a young child. But beginning around the age of eight, fears become reality based. By this time, children have enough life experiences to know that bad things actually happen. During school-age years, many children fear something terrible might happen to loved ones or they themselves might die. But these children also have the ability to logically plan solutions when faced with problems.

Our high level of media immersion exposes children to a multitude of frightening screen images. Graphic elements that are physically close—such as a murder shown on a handheld game—may be especially scary as

〉〉〉

When my boys were five-year-old twins, they saw Home Alone *at Grandma's house. Ever since, they've been worried someone will come and "steal" them at night. Before bed we check all the windows and the locks on the doors.*

A year later they still ask, "What if a bad guy breaks a window?" I have no other answer for them except to say that God is watching, too. We read a comforting Psalm, and they are content to go to sleep—but they still insist on checking the window latch.

Marianne, mother of three

they invade a child's perimeter of personal space. Continually monitor all forms of media, including news programs and commercials. If gory or violent images appear, turn off the screen. When appropriate, briefly explain the situation that was shown. If your child appears shaken, physically put your arm around him. Feeling your touch can be very comforting, even to an older child.

As children become more mature in their thinking and more risk aware, give them a script to follow in specific situations. Instead of a generic, "Now be careful while we're at the mall," say, "If someone ever reaches for you, pull away and yell, 'You're not my mom!'" Some parents and children actually practice these "safe kid" scenarios. Physically acting out possible situations is one way to emphasize the importance of staying alert for a child who seems oblivious to dangers. However, a child who is easily frightened may have bad dreams if you dwell on scary topics. You are the expert on your child. Apply that knowledge to every situation so your child becomes risk aware without being fearful.

〉〉〉 26

Rookie Target

〉 *What is it?*

First time mom, a focal point for marketers.

〉 *Why should I care?*

Women who are pregnant for the first time are primary marketing targets. Companies know that expectant moms belong to a powerful demographic. Rookie moms not only invest heavily as they prepare for the birth of their child, but they will also spend an increasing amount of money on family products in the future.

Although brand loyalty has decreased, marketers still anticipate that if a woman buys a product during her first pregnancy, she will continue to buy from the company. This "crib to grave" strategy is a reason marketers shadow first timers. Companies want to know where they go, who they talk to, and what they do. This is why infant product companies seek personal information from rookie moms. Baby magazines and children's stores run frequent contests and sponsor giveaways to capture personal information including: name, address, e-mail, delivery date, and so on.

Strategic marketers know that rookie moms have multifaceted lives. They are busy. They have many circles of influence, and companies want to tag along. Here's why: If everyone at the Lamaze class requests the recipe for a snack a mom bought, that mom becomes the brand evangelist for those ingredients. Or, if a mom at a MOPS group talks about a pregnancy Web site, others listen. After all, opinions from friends have more credibility than any advertisement.

Authenticity, or realness, is important to today's moms. And because women are relational, they don't merely use a product, they talk about it! This is an example of what's called buzz marketing. Marketers want first-time expectant women to generate buzz about their products. Rookie targets have emerged as effective "human media."

〉〉〉

The first time I bought a maternity shirt from the "Motherhood" store, I was asked at least 10 questions about my pregnancy, due date, whether I was planning to breastfeed or not, and so on while the cashier entered my answers into her computer. Then when I got home, I realized that in the bag with the shirt were samples and advertisements on everything from a "mommy" Ensure drink, to diapers, to belly lotion!

Ana, mother of one

The Internet has created a browsing-buying pattern that has increased the effectiveness of rookie targets. Known as Web-to-store shopping, people research products online before buying in brick and mortar stores. Because moms spend so much time e-mailing and participating in Weblogs and chat rooms, the buzz created by rookie targets can quickly and dramatically increase product sales.

〉 What can I do?

Rookie moms are on a rapidly accelerating learning curve. They are eager for information and open to input. Be alert for these strategies designed specifically to attract rookie targets. Awareness of these concepts can help moms stick to a budget and avoid impulse buys.

1. Rookie moms prioritize convenience, balance, family health, and child enrichment. That's why advertising highlights these themes. Advertising is written to emotionally connect with the rookie target and propel her to purchase the product.

2. Suggestive selling is extremely successful with rookie targets because their level of experience is low and the level of need is high. Here's a sample: If you buy a sippy cup on a Web site, you might be asked if you also need baby bibs which pop up on the next screen. A veteran mom might wonder suspiciously, *What are they trying to sell me now?* A new mom might appreciate the suggestion and admit, *I didn't think of that.*

3. Moms are online 24/7. Many parent-targeted chat room hits come during the night. Companies provide three elements on their Web sites specifically to meet the needs of rookie targets: content (moms are

eager to learn); community (moms tend to feel lonely, plus hormones during pregnancy can intensify emotions); and commerce (first-time moms need a wide variety of products). Be especially alert to these three connecting points if you are shopping in the middle of the night. Bookmark a potential purchase to recheck in the morning when you are more awake.

4. Before buying anything that promises to save you time, think through how you'll use the product. Consider whether the time you might save is worth the money.

27

Schedule Gridlock

》 What is it?

Calendar overload that prioritizes children's activities instead of relationships.

》 Why should I care?

Parents who want what's best for their children have the most extracurricular and enrichment options in history. From martial arts to tuba, and drama to spelling bees, children and parents have a full range of choices. In our risk-aware society, organized activities have emerged as a security-driven choice for children. After all, it's safer for a child to chase after a ball with nine other kids on a public field than to play video games down the street at a neighbor's house.

Concern about school cliques and classroom bullies has propelled parents to seek peer socialization for their child beyond the school community. Children who participate in activities outside the immediate area can work as a team member, learn cooperation, and practice skills beyond the shadow of playground taunts.

And so for these and many more valid reasons, calendars are color-coded and carpool drivers chauffeur kids. But activity overload hovers over this scenario. Parents attempt to cram all of life's extras into the only available hours: weeknights and weekends. As a result, going to places instead of seeing people is what matters. Organized activities take priority over personal relationships. The result is schedule gridlock.

〉 What can I do?

Before signing up for an activity, ask your child two questions: Do you want to do this? Does this sound like fun?

Ask yourself two questions: What are the goals for my child? Is this activity a good way for my child to meet those goals?

Often, these basic questions are avoided. Instead parents first look for activities that fit into a specific time block or locate a class that fits

〉〉〉

My child's best friend in high school worked at McDonald's, drilled in ROTC, and also participated in forensics. I wondered when he ever slept. When I asked, he replied, "Sleep? What's that?"

Tim, father of one

into the most convenient carpool. The line between unhealthy pushing and healthy encouraging blurs when activities, not the needs of the child or family, become the driver.

In a conscientious and sincere effort to expose children to a wide range of activities, busyness can quickly replace family time. Activity commitments can substitute for downtime, both for a parent and child. Be alert to signs of activity overload: a child moving in slow motion when it's time to leave home; homework getting crammed into a few moments before bedtime; a lack of eagerness or enthusiasm; falling asleep in the car; and so on.

Time famine results from schedule gridlock. To assess whether or not this is happening in your family, focus on a single aspect of the activity merry-go-round: record car time associated with your children's activities for a single week. Note minutes spent loading, unloading, driving, and waiting. At the end of seven days, add up the minutes. Did your child spend more time looking at the back of your head while you drove than talking with you face to face? If so, consider taking these steps to reduce the schedule gridlock:

1. Substitute family events for solo activities. For example, instead of having your child on soccer, gymnastics, and swim teams, your child might join you at family swim and leave the swim team.

2. Set seasonal limits. For example, you might determine that one sport and one enrichment activity is the maximum for each child every season. That means a child can continue piano lessons, but must choose between volleyball and ballet.

3. Consider the investment. Begin with time. Include practices, rehearsals, games, driving time, recitals, classes, and fund-raising efforts. Make a similar, comprehensive list when considering costs: uniforms,

tournament fees, league costs, snacks, and so on. Detailed, advance planning helps put the commitment into perspective.

When examining the family calendar, separate planned play from free play, which the child directs himself. Every child needs unstructured time. He needs time to dream and to not perform, to hang out and not learn something, to relax and not go anywhere. If necessary, designate "time-outs" on the calendar. Spending time together as a family is one of the most effective ways to defeat schedule gridlock. For more guidance on this important topic, see the excellent book *Home Court Advantage*, by Dr. Kevin Leman.

28

Smorgasbord Surfer

> ### › What is it?

A child faced with numerous choices.

> ### › Why should I care?

Children receive messages through multiple channels, and the options expand with the adoption of each new technology. Today's children belong to the thumb generation, because children access so many choices through their thumbs. A starter list includes cell phones, movies, iPods, Internet, cable, and satellite TV. And yet, those are merely a few options for *receiving* the information; they don't even include the actual information.

But children are informed consumers. Almost all kids watch TV and read magazines. A high percentage of children listen to the radio, play video games, and see movies. They know what's available. They know what they like, but that doesn't necessarily help them make wise choices.

For example, when shopping, children notice promotions. They notice innovation. They are drawn to three-dimensional objects, so they'll see shelf signage that extends into the aisle. They gravitate toward displays with motion. Obviously, what attracts children and might ultimately be their choice can be unrelated to the actual product. A child might pick a specific bubble bath because of an in-store display, not because the moisturizer will smooth dry skin. In a smorgasbord world, the best or the best for you may not even get noticed. When faced with so many choices, some kids simply shrug and move on. Others get side-tracked by a glitzy ad or celebrity endorsement. Still others are so over-whelmed they decide by default; they delay until someone decides for them. Yet the dizzying array of choices children face makes the process of decision-making an invaluable life skill. Options may entice, but how can children learn to choose wisely?

❭ What can I do?

Decision-making is a skill that is learned, and parents must be the teachers. Children learn to make informed choices through practice and modeling, not osmosis.

A five-step process can be simplified for young children and used for a child of any age:

1. Clarify the choices.
2. Weigh the options.

3. Make a decision.

4. After living with the choice, reassess.

5. Adapt or change as necessary.

Even young children are surrounded by choices, so start by teaching preschoolers. Ask a three year old, "Do you want to wear a red shirt or a blue shirt?" Ask a four year old, "Do you want to pick up your toys before or after snack time?" Choice allows an element of control. Children, especially preschoolers, don't control very much in their lives. That's why making choices is so empowering for them. However, because children often overestimate their abilities, parents must offer age-appropriate options.

Occasionally, children will not have the information or experience necessary to make a decision. For example, a child attending her first sleepover may not know what she actually needs to pack, so a parent helps her make a list. At this point, the parent might help her daughter lay out pajama options and delete them, one by one. In this situation,

When I was a child, I can recall seeing only two after-school TV shows aimed at kids, Mr. Rogers and Captain Kangaroo. By the time my son came along, you could find at least one program going at any time from 6:00 A.M. to 7:00 P.M. on cable —and often there were two or more to choose from at any given hour. My wife and I had to pick carefully the one or two programs a day that we would let him watch.

Stan, father of one

the parent walked with her daughter through the many choices to make a final decision.

Adult modeling is most valuable to children when our actions and behaviors are linked together. For example, when faced with a stopped-up sink, a child hears us verbalize our choices: "I can get that home repair book and see if I can figure out what the problem is . . . or I can call Grandpa when he gets home from work . . . or I can call the plumber." The child watches how we approach the problem and think through possible solutions.

Kids are truly smorgasbord surfers: They *expect* to be offered multiple choices. However, the real world also includes no-option situations. A three year old should not be allowed to choose his bedtime. A disobedient 10 year old should not be allowed to choose his punishment. A teen driver does not have the option of wearing his seat belt. Although a child might assume he always has at least one choice, children must learn to accept the unpopular reality: Even in a smorgasbord society, sometimes we don't have options.

29

Summer Slide

The decline of a child's academic skills during the traditional summer vacation from school.

Summer learning loss has affected generations of students who do not attend school during June, July, and August. The greatest loss occurs among low-income students and those who struggle academically during the school year.

In a typical classroom, teachers spend at least the first quarter of each school year reviewing material from the previous grade. In many locations, this "review season" continues until children return to school after the Christmas holidays.

Although the summer slide is not new, societal shifts and recent attempts to solve the problem have triggered heightened awareness. The current "standards movement" demands accountability among teachers and learners. As a result, issues including the summer slide and social promotion (when a student is moved ahead with his class, regardless of his academic performance) have captured headlines.

To prevent skill loss during the summer, some schools have modified the calendar so that classroom breaks are shorter. For example, some schools evenly distribute vacation days through 12 months, resulting in a year-round school. However, this approach often results in parents' scrambling for short-term extended day care. Most attempts to add days to school calendars have failed. Observers attribute this to parents who want children to have fun during the summer, lobbying by various amusement and leisure industries, and concern about student and faculty fatigue.

To limit learning loss, schools now prepare required reading lists to be completed during summer months. Educational programs are increasingly offered during the summer through public libraries, camps, school libraries, churches, and community agencies. Formats may vary, but both remedial and enrichment opportunities have increased.

〉 What can I do?

Plan for summer before the school year ends. Begin by talking with your child's teacher. Identify academic areas of strength and weakness. Ask your child to list areas of interest. If appropriate, work together to set some general goals. Next, look for programs and activities that match those goals. Summer instruction in small groups or individual settings produces the best results.

Help your child complete his required summer reading list by providing a supportive environment. Build reading time into a daily routine. For example, if you eat supper together, read immediately after supper (before washing the dishes!), or begin the bedtime routine 20 minutes early to allow for family reading time.

Summer learning loss is even greater in math than in reading. Look for opportunities to practice math skills. For example, you can easily involve your child in financial transactions using currency. This is especially important for children who live in a world of virtual cash. Here's a sample for summer practice:

- A preschooler can accept the change offered from a clerk. Ask your child to identify each coin.
- A seven or eight year old can count the change to verify the correct amount. Then put the change in your coat pocket, and ask him to identify the coins simply by touch.

Beyond buying educational software and strategy-based board games, I pay my children to read during the summer. The little ones get 5 cents per page of challenging reading; the older receive up to 5 cents a page (I pay more for nonfiction).

Meredith, mother of 3

- A 10 year old can order and buy her own lunch without adult assistance.
- A 12 year old can calculate the tip.

Although a program of intentional summer learning can prevent dramatic academic loss, be realistic about what your child can accomplish: Even intensive summer programs may not compensate for limited learning during the regular school year. Yet for children to compete successfully in a global economy, parents must take action to stop the summer slide.

>>> 30

Tech Tether

> What is it?

A high-tech communication device that links parent and child. For example, a cell phone.

> Why should I care?

Tech tethering has been triggered by parental concern for children's safety. For years, webcams have allowed parents to see what their child is eating at daycare and what he's doing at summer camp. But that generalized monitoring has been enhanced by child-specific tracking devices. As a result, even young children carry cell phones. Many are child-sized, with a simple keypad and easy-to-use features. Speed dials link children directly to parents.

Safety is the underlying factor in school-based tracking systems.

Tags with microchips and tiny antennae clip onto backpacks; others are inserted into standard-issue student ID cards worn on a lanyard. Signals indicate when a child leaves a secure area or the school grounds.

Parents of older teens appreciate the monitoring devices installed in cars. This is especially helpful during emergencies. Yet on an everyday basis, these systems offer the ultimate in backseat driving. Information about driving habits—including whether or not the driver wears a seat belt and is driving within the speed limit—can be transmitted immediately to Mom and Dad. Interactive elements even allow a parent to remotely disable a car after it's stopped.

Other devices allow parents to signal that their young driver needs to slow down. But teens refer to location-aware technology as a leash; the expanded use of the "nanny cam" concept has also been labeled parent spyware. The terms are probably accurate; after all, geography no longer limits adult supervision for a toddler in a nursery or a teen after a foot-

〉〉〉

My teen daughter knows that if she gets a cell phone, I'll use it to find out where she is and may curtail some of her freedom. She resisted getting one until she and her father were separated in a Washington, D.C., museum for more than half an hour—during which time they were both pretty nervous. "It never would have happened," she said, "if we both had cell phones." Now she's asking for a cell phone for Christmas and is even willing to pay the monthly fee.

Anne, mother of three

ball game. And that's precisely the point: Tech tracking, sometimes called "helicoptering," allows a parent to hover.

Schools, churches, and other organizations have policies that limit or strictly define use of cell phones or other technology that can be used for tracking. However, parents must consider the implications of tech tethering on a child's emotional growth. Can a child develop independence while parent spyware hovers?

⟩ What can I do?

Before installing location-aware technology in the car or purchasing a cell phone for a nine year old, determine the purpose. For example, a parent-child discussion about a cell phone typically focuses on anticipated use, cost, and features. Those questions are fairly clear cut. Responses generally reflect age-influenced expectations. A younger child might view a phone as a cool bonus; for a tween, a sign of growing independence and parent trust; for a teen, a basic necessity.

However, a parent would also need to consider:

- In what ways would a cell phone increase my effectiveness as a parent?
- If my child gets a cell phone, how would our patterns of family communication change? (Will we continue to prioritize face time? Will my child still learn to read my body language? What will I lose by not seeing my child when he talks to me?)
- How would a cell phone affect my child's decision-making ability?
- Would it decrease or increase my child's emotional dependence?

- How does a child's cell phone fit into our family definition of materialism?
- Would a cell phone delay my "letting go"?

Similar questions must be answered when choosing any type of monitoring system. Different formats may be more effective than others during various seasons of family life. Children and parents may have a higher comfort factor with certain systems.

Microchip technology has increased the ease of child monitoring, but now parents must find a comfortable balance between high- and low-tech monitoring. Children need to be watched, but they also need to move toward independence. They need to become self-reliant while we gradually step back from the everyday details of their lives. How does tech-tracking fit into that picture? That's the key question parents must answer for themselves.

Tech Trades

> *What is it?*

The substitution of tech-based skills for traditional life skills.

> *Why should I care?*

Your child may be keyboard literate, but can he tie his shoe? Generations of children learned to tie by making bunny ears with shoestring loops. Today, children zip Velcro. Can your child tell time from a dial clock? Or can he only rattle off numerals from a digital screen?

Tying a shoe and telling time from a dial are just two of the minor life skills that have been buried or lost under the tech deluge.

Children aren't the only victims of tech trade-offs. We can bake a potato in five minutes, e-mail a prescription refill and pick it up without leaving the car, and simply click to find the right song on a bedtime

CD. Yet, even using tech time savers, parents are time starved. Technology *should* save us time, but are we tech rich and time famished?

Microchip technology will continue to define and shape our lives. But as we adopt each new invention, we must continually ask, "Is tech taking away or adding to my child's life?" The list goes on forever as we document ways tech affects our lives. When technology substitutes for important life skills, we must teach our children those skills.

⟩ What can I do?

Replace what's being lost.

For example, video games and computers dominate available downtime for children. As a result, some fail to learn basic social skills, including making eye contact and reading body language.

⟩ ⟩ ⟩

While we have a good array of home computer equipment and software, we don't have PowerPoint, a lack that caused big problems when our twin boys suddenly seemed to be assigned an e-presentation every other week. Computer crashes and last-minute data crises turned the simple act of gathering and reporting information into desperate searches for anybody with an available computer. We all learned a lot more about who had dependable PowerPoint than the geography or English topic at hand.

Liz, mother of two

The next time you speak with your child, intentionally make eye contact throughout the conversation. Does your child look straight back at you? Can he understand your body language? Model and practice interpersonal communication skills with your child. To practice eye contact, avoid talking with your child unless you are looking each other in the eye. That will dramatically decrease the number of times you call across the house and also give your child practice in maintaining eye contact. To practice reading body language, play the game, "Guess what I feel" by posing your body in different ways. For example, cross your arms and look mean, reach out for a hug with a smile, and so on. Children avoid learning either of these skills when "talking" online.

Tech trades have also dramatically changed children's ability to write effectively. Instant messaging and text messaging on cell phones have created an entirely new language. Some refer to this as "IM Fingo" (instant message lingo using fingers), "kidspeek," or the more specific term, "computer-mediated communication" (CMC). Regardless of the terminology, kids write using emoticons (keyboard characters that convey feelings) and shortcuts (abbreviations using letters). A typical online conversation includes both emoticons like this :>) (smile) and shortcuts like brb (be right back) or ttyl (talk to you later).

Language arts teachers admit that tech-savvy kids use IM Fingo so frequently that the new language sneaks into formal compositions. As a result, school assignments can be a combination of formal English, Fingo, and emoticons.

At home, students should be encouraged to proofread homework and handwritten letters. Children might also need a reminder to use online spell checkers before submitting a typed assignment. Children can get everyday practice using formal written language when you dictate a shopping list. Or, ask your child to write the reminders that are posted on the refrigerator. And when you communicate online, model accurate spelling and correct grammar.

Among parents, a major tech trade is poly-tasking, or doing simultaneous tasks including ones that involve technology. That means you poly-task when you answer the cell phone, spread peanut butter for a hungry three year old, and pour ingredients into the bread maker, all at the same time. This is just one example of a tech trade that affects parents. We need to be alert to the trade-offs we make, as some occur almost automatically. We must continually ask, "Do tech trade-offs decrease my effectiveness as a parent or help me parent more effectively?"

⟩⟩⟩ 32

Third Parent

⟩ *What is it?*

Media.

⟩ *Why should I care?*

Media have become a third parent. Bedtime is arranged around a favorite television program. Family conversations are cut short when a cell phone rings. Homework is set aside until a video game ends. In many families, media decide what children will do and when they will do it.

Children consume media in increasing amounts. That's to be expected as new media are more attractive and affordable than ever before. High-tech toys and tools are so easy to use that even a three year old can click and point to enter a playground as big as the world.

Some media usage is good, even incredible. A child can be fascinated as a flower opens in slow motion on a video screen. Tears will run down Grandma's cheek as she views an e-mailed photo of the newest family member less than an hour after birth. And parents breathe a sigh of relief when global positioning pinpoints the location of their teen driver who hydroplaned. Media *are* incredible.

But when allowed, media can be invasive. Television sends 12 year olds unhealthy messages about alcohol. An anonymous cyber bully destroys an entire school year for a fifth-grade victim. Magazines promote unrealistic body images to teenagers. Media messages enter homes through a growing number of portals.

Media can't, and shouldn't be, stopped. However, the power of media must be reduced. Television, the Internet, cell phones, and other forms of digital media cannot be allowed to continue as a third parent.

〉 What can I do?

Media education begins at home. After the age of two, a toddler might watch a brief program. Many baby DVDs include multiple, 10-minute programs on a single disk. The length is intentional: Ten minutes is an appropriate amount of time for a baby. These short-format programs often invite children to physically respond or react to what's on the screen. Get up and move with your child. Sing along. Talk about what you're watching, then turn off the screen. This parent-child activity is called co-viewing.

As your baby grows up, decide what role you want media to play in your family life. Start by gathering information. Make a media diary or journal. Simply put a pencil and pad of paper at each screen in the house. Every time that tech toy is used during a single week, record the start and stop time. At the end of the week, add up the minutes. Then decide: Do media play an appropriate role in our family?

If you want to delete the third parent from your family, begin by setting limits. Limit the number of media portals and the amount of time media are used. That might mean you donate extra televisions to the community rummage sale or give away a video game console.

Some families with elementary-school-aged children follow these five guidelines:

1. Turn on the TV only when a four-eyed monster (parent and child) is viewing.

2. Use a single, adult-sized remote control.

3. Highlight appropriate programs when the weekly TV guide arrives. Turn on the television only at these times.

4. Don't allow eating when the television is on or a child is using a cell phone, video game, or computer. Media are a factor in childhood obesity.

It's easy to think we're having quality time if our son is sitting on our lap at the computer screen, but that's not always the case. We have to police the electronic part of our household because we can be interacting with the computer instead of each other.

Janis, mother of one

5. Tape programs for later viewing. Because even ads and previews can include offensive language and inappropriate behaviors, use tech aids to allow time shifting and selective viewing. Monitoring media is a daily challenge, which is easier when the television, video game, or computer is centrally located.

As you observe your child's use of media, be alert to your own media patterns. Children copy parents. That means that if you're a channel surfer, your child might become one too.

Consider ways to use media as a bridge to other activities. Often, after only a few moments of co-viewing, your child will respond positively if you offer to read a book or play catch. Be especially alert to seasons when screens morph into electronic wallpaper. The number of child-sized couch potatoes often peaks during summer months and school vacations.

>>> 33

Togethering

> What is it?

The emotional connection between family members, known as parent-child bonding in previous generations.

> Why should I care?

"Togethering" is one of the most important elements of parenting. But togethering has edged into an at-risk category. Due to a number of current societal factors, the transition from preschool to the primary grades is one of the most critical periods for intentional togethering.

Follow this scenario:

A three year old snuggles in for bedtime stories, prayers, and perhaps a few songs before going to sleep. Nighttime is a gentle bridge from the busyness of the day to the peace of a restful sleep. But as children move into organized activities, bedtime becomes chaotic. A six year old has entered the season of schedule gridlock. Any free time is filled with edutainment, although a child sometimes gets sidetracked by kidad clutter. And when a seven year old returns home from after-school soccer practice, there's barely time to clean up, do a little homework, and eat before bedtime. As a result, togethering slips away in the busyness of life. This happens fairly consistently, even though parents prioritize family.

Although the daily peak of togethering is traditionally at bedtime, emotional connections should continue throughout the day. Even when time famine threatens, parents can recapture the togethering that contributes to a family-centric foundation.

〉 What can I do?

Define togethering for your family. Although the definition changes as families move from the early years through the school-age years to the tween years, the concept is a constant. Decide what makes good parent-

〉〉〉

There's nothing like that time early in the morning when my daughter pads downstairs to sit with me before the sun comes up. I'm usually getting a head start on e-mail or making the coffee, but she always greets me with a hug and we'll snuggle on the couch. No matter what might happen the rest of the day, there's never anything that can top that.

Mick, father of two

child time for your family now. Do you define togethering as quality time in which you totally focus on your child? Or does togethering time count on your emotional register if your child accompanies you to the store? When you clearly define the concept, you will find it easier to meet your goal.

Families who prioritize togethering successfully fight societal clutter. Identify touchpoints that will help you regroup as a family. Look for places and time blocks where you relate to your child as an individual. For example, you might transform one room into an e-free (entertainment-free) zone. Or make the hour after supper m-free (media free). Distractions detract from togethering.

As you seek to refocus on your family, look critically at the calendar. The daily pace accelerates during three seasons: Falloween, the beginning of summer, and back to school (BTS). Your child needs even more emotional support during these transitions and busy seasons. Prioritize togethering at these times.

Although some observers blame tech immersion for the decline of togethering, that's an unfair assessment. Selectively integrate technology into daily activities to claim more time with your child. Here's an updated example of the classic "six steps to bed" routine that generations of parents and children have used to bond.

1. Prequel: Turn off all screens at least an hour before bedtime. Some research indicates that the artificial light from monitors can "trick" the body into thinking it's daytime instead of night.

2. Brush teeth: A variety of electric toothbrushes are sized especially for younger children. Some high-tech brushes have ergonomic handles, oscillating heads, and other kid-friendly features. Because kids think

tech is cool, avoid the "Do I have to brush?" arguments with high-tech brushes and you'll have a few extra moments for togethering.

3. Bathe: Although aromatherapy is a current fad, additives can irritate some children's skin. But a soothing bath, perhaps with a few toys, offers precious togethering opportunities in a busy day.

4. Cuddle: The sense of touch, so vital to an infant, continues to be important as a child grows up. However, today's parenting-on-the-go means some children suffer from "skin hunger," or the desire for more physical closeness. A calming cuddle not only settles a child for sleep, but also meets this critical need for being held. Tweens need hugs, too. Just be alert to your child's sensitivity about her changing body.

5. Read: Children's software and various Web sites offer bedtime stories, but whenever possible, read an actual book with your child. Proposing that the first one in bed gets to choose an extra book can eliminate stalling.

6. Talk: Some parents help a child practice short-term memory skills by reviewing what happened during the day. Praying together is also a good way to close the day's events and help your child feel restful and at peace.

Create your own bedtime ritual to provide a gentle end to a day of togethering!

〉〉〉

One way a parent and child can bond emotionally and spiritually is to pray together. Whenever possible, my wife and I would pray with our daughters at bedtime. It bonds a child with her parents when they pray together and later see how God answers their prayers.

Ronald, father of three

>>> 34

Undercover Advertising

> What is it?

In-school marketing targeted to students.

> Why should I care?

Advertising is all around us. Media commentary has even highlighted "embedded ads." This is intentional product placement in television or movies. For example, when watching TV, a favorite brand of pop might be on a table in a sitcom, or a character will shop at a specific store during a film.

But your child might be exposed to a more targeted breed of undercover advertising through the classroom. This commonly begins in childcare with preschoolers and continues through high school. As a result, an alphabet border featuring cars and trucks on the day care wall might have come from a vehicle manufacturer, and the school cafeteria posters may show snack foods.

Loyalty programs are common in schools. For example, student families might save product labels that fund purchases for the school. Corporations also negotiate vending contracts, which create revenue streams for both the school and company. Businesses buy advertising in school newspapers and provide ad-splashed book covers. Corporate-developed curriculum often includes state of the art video components, teaching guides, and posters. Of course, company logos identify the source, and products are often integrated in the material.

These corporate donations are generous. Schools that face a budget crunch welcome standards-based curriculum. Coaches seek sponsors for fifth-grade basketball uniforms. Teachers, who typically fund classroom extras "out of pocket," often embrace commercially sponsored programs. Young students delight in seeing familiar logos and branded images. In many situations, extracurricular activities would be limited without corporate donations.

But because children are growing up in a world of commercial

>>>

When I went to high school, the halls and lunchrooms had handmade signs promoting the upcoming pep rally or spring prom. In my son's high school, the signs are now professionally done and promote Coke products and the selling points of a particular technical college.

Larry, father of one

immersion, some social commentators suggest making schools ad-free. Some parents feel that inviting advertisers into school merely postpones a long-term financial solution. Other parents would prefer to pay for non-core programs (sports, theater, music, etc.) than have their children exposed to commercials in the classroom. As a result, undercover advertising in schools has emerged as a controversial issue.

〉 What can I do?

Check your parent handbook for the policy on in-school marketing. Then ask the school administrator about current participation in corporate-sponsored programs. When you've gathered complete and accurate information, determine your personal comfort level with the undercover advertising that reaches your child. Then express your sentiments through appropriate channels.

If you are uncomfortable with the type or amount of advertising that reaches your child, suggest less invasive commercialism or other funding sources. For example, a corporate sponsor for the basketball team might be willing to substitute an acknowledgment at a single game instead of having the company name printed on each player's uniform. Or, instead of seeing corporate logos splashed on the gym scoreboard and the cafeteria wall, perhaps a company would "adopt a school" in a program that matches company employees with students through mentoring and career education situations.

Parents of younger children should pay special attention to undercover advertising. Until second grade, children are especially susceptible to advertising messages. A fifth grader will understand that a logo-splashed book cover is simply another form of advertising, but a first grader will simply absorb the messages without questioning their validity.

Also, don't assume that a product is good just because the school benefits from corporate donations. Although "returnship" (corporate involvement with community organizations) can be productive, ethical, and positive for everyone, a school-business relationship is not necessarily an educational endorsement or a comment on quality.

As undercover advertising through in-school marketing receives more attention, stay alert to legislative and local conversations so your voice is heard.

Urban Legends

› What is it?

Fiction, with or without an element of truth, told as fact.

› Why should I care?

The concept of urban legends is not new, but two key elements have reshaped this trend into a relevant topic for families: cyberspace and young children with Internet access.

In past years, stories told as facts circulated among adults. The far-fetched fiction occasionally drifted down to teens, but rarely, if ever, reached young children. However, because even young children use cyberspace as their playground, five and six year olds are being exposed to urban legends. Both lies and truths spread quickly on the Internet.

In addition, technology continues to create ideas and products only imagined in the past. Urban legends with incredible content no longer seem so unbelievable. This is true especially in content areas which relate to security issues and touch at fears. We're raising children in an era when the threat of nuclear, biological, and chemical weapons is a real and ever-present danger. Our country, our city, even our homes no longer seem untouchable. It's harder to separate fact from fiction. Today the warning "Urban Legends Ahead" is appropriately directed to parents and children, especially when they hear questions like these:

- Are snakes crawling in the playland ball pit at the local fast-food restaurant?
- Could that fake tattoo on your eight year old's arm be laced with an illicit drug?
- Will Halloween candy from the neighbor contain a razor blade?
- Is a kidnapping ring working out of the hardware store?

Questions like these spread especially quickly because they trigger fear. In contrast, some urban legends drift lazily through conversations, over a period of months or years, when they contain embarrassing stories or obvious misinformation without any relation to truth. However, in either case, parents should take every opportunity to assist children in developing their own personal truth filter through which they can distinguish fact from fiction.

〉 What can I do?

"Don't believe everything you hear" is good advice. But for a child under the age of eight who can't differentiate between what's real and what's not, that caution is merely a starting point. Whenever possible, use concrete examples to disprove urban legends.

For example, suppose your kindergartener comes home from school and asks, "Daddy, is there a giant alligator in the sewer in front of our house?" Often, a question like this will contain an undercurrent of fear. Treat this fear as real; the concern is real to her. After showing respect for her feelings, some parents use humor to emphasize the truth. For example, Dad might ask, "Can you imagine an alligator here? With all the snow on the ground, he'd need a tall pair of boots."

Or use humor as a transition to information. "Only a silly alligator would live here. He'd need a coat. Let's go to the computer and see what we can find about where alligators really live." This general template, beginning with a lightening of the mood, followed by a serious response to an urban legend and an opportunity to teach facts, can be adapted to many urban legends. You will determine the most effective approach for your child and situation.

Help older children independently determine the accuracy of "information." Encourage them to consider the source, especially if they've read

— 〉〉〉 ———————————————————

Initially, urban legends cause a gullability problem because too many people believe them. That only lasts until nobody believes anything! Violence influences kids. Sex influences kids. But because urban legends are a more subtle influence, a cynical wall can form in a child's mind during what should be the age of innocence.

Steven, father of one

a forwarded e-mail. Fear or genuine concern may motivate an intelligent friend to pass along a believable story. This happens among children and adults.

Show your children how you apply your personal filter of good judgment. There are several Web sites that offer information on fact versus fiction. You might want to plug "urban legends" into an online search engine and try to verify what's real and what's not before passing on a possible rumor.

Some hoaxes are related to illnesses or medical conditions that affect children. Because a child's health is a top priority, hearing a horror story about a drug reaction could trigger nightmares for any caring parent. Don't withhold prescribed medication or delay a scheduled vaccination for your child based on a virtual report or hearsay from a carpool driver. Instead, get the facts from a health care professional who knows your child. Consult experts you trust to help separate fact from fiction.

When you hear an urban legend, stop the tall tale. Don't pass it along. If the information is newsworthy, legitimate organizations or institutions will publish the complete and accurate story.

Notes

Chapter Three

1. "Marketers Take Note: Young People Are Looking for Social, Political Causes to Get Behind," Youth Markets Alert, vol. XVI, no. 10, October 1, 2004.

Chapter Twelve

1. Christina Hoff Sommers, "Enough already with kid gloves," *USA Today*, June 1, 2005, http://www.usatoday.com/news/opinion/editorials/2005-05-31-kid-gloves-edit_x.htm (accessed October 13, 2005).

Chapter Thirteen

1. Mayer on Marketing, EPM Communications, March 1, 2005.

Chapter Nineteen

1. Sally Squires, "To Eat Better, Eat Together," *Washington Post*, March 1, 2005.

2. Bruce Horovitz quoting Phil Lempert, "A whole new ballgame in grocery shopping," *USA Today*, March 8, 2005, http://www.usatoday.com/printedition/money/20050309/whole foods.art.htm (accessed November 1, 2005).

3. Nancy Cole, "Set an example for your kids by eating right, exercising," http://www.ediets.com/news/article.cfm/cmi_1467357/cid_32 (accessed November 10, 2005).

Chapter Twenty-Three

1. John D. Solomon, "What's Indecent?" *USA Today*, February 9, 2005.

FOCUS ON THE FAMILY®

Welcome to the family!

Whether you purchased this book, borrowed it, or received it as a gift, we're glad you're reading it. It's just one of the many helpful, encouraging, and biblically based resources produced by Focus on the Family for people in all stages of life.

Focus began in 1977 with the vision of one man, Dr. James Dobson, a licensed psychologist and author of numerous best-selling books on marriage, parenting, and family. Alarmed by the societal, political, and economic pressures that were threatening the existence of the American family, Dr. Dobson founded Focus on the Family with one employee and a once-a-week radio broadcast aired on 36 stations.

Now an international organization reaching millions of people daily, Focus on the Family is dedicated to preserving values and strengthening and encouraging families through the life-changing message of Jesus Christ.

Focus on the Family Magazines

These faith-building, character-developing publications address the interests, issues, concerns, and challenges faced by every member of your family from preschool through the senior years.

| Focus on the Family **Citizen®** U.S. news issues | Focus on the Family **Clubhouse Jr.™** Ages 4 to 8 | Focus on the Family **Clubhouse™** Ages 8 to 12 | **Breakaway®** Teen guys | **Brio®** Teen girls 12 to 16 | **Brio & Beyond®** Teen girls 16 to 19 | **Plugged In®** Reviews movies, music, TV |

FOR MORE INFORMATION

 Online:
Log on to www.family.org
In Canada, log on to www.focusonthefamily.ca

 Phone:
Call toll free: (800) A-FAMILY (232-6459)
In Canada, call toll free: (800) 661-9800

Guide Your Children With Confidence
from Focus on the Family ®

Delight in Your Child's Design
Do you have a child with some challenging personality traits? Aspects of a child's personality can frustrate or discourage even good parents. This book enriches the parent-child relationship by helping you understand and appreciate the unique design, temperament, and abilities of your children. Paperback.

Giving Your Child the Excellence Edge
Give your child an extra edge for success, both now and in the future. Written by a mother and teacher who has seen these principles work, Giving Your Child the Excellence Edge defines 10 essential traits and shows you how to build these qualities in your children — and yourself. Paperback.

Home Court Advantage
Many well-meaning parents, hoping to give their children a head start on the competition, overload their children's schedules, and fragment family time. Best-selling author and psychologist Dr. Kevin Leman shows how to reclaim your role as the primary influence on your child by enjoying time together and making indelible, life-shaping memories. Hardcover.

•   •   •